Beckett Great Sports Heroes

Anfernee Hardaway

By the staff of Beckett Publications

House of Collectibles • New York

H This is a registered trademark of Random House, Inc.

Published by: House of Collectibles
201 East 50th Street
New York, NY 10022

Distributed by Ballantine Books, a division of Random House, Inc., New York,
and simultaneously in Canada by Random House of Canada Limited, Toronto.

Manufactured in the United States of America
ISBN: 0-676-60033-6
LC #96-77474

Cover design by Michaelis & Carpelis Design Associates, Inc.

Cover photo by Rocky Widner

First Edition: August 1996

10   9   8   7   6   5   4   3   2   1

The Publisher would like to thank Dr. James Beckett
and the staff of Beckett Publications for providing the editorial and photo content of this book.

Managing Editor Rudy J. Klancnik and Art Director Jeff Stanton had the able editorial, design and production assistance of
Barbara Barry, Rob Barry, Therese Bellar, Amy Brougher, Emily Camp, Belinda Cross, Randy Cummings, Marlon DePaula, Eric Evans, Barbara Faraldo,
Mary Gonzalez-Davis, Tracy Hackler, Brent Hawkins, Paul Kerutis, Benedito Leme, Sara Leeman, Lori Lindsey, Sara Maneval, Louis Marroquin, Mike McAllister,
Lisa McQuilkin Monaghan, Daniel Moscoso Jr., Randy Mosty, Lisa O'Neill, Mike Pagel, Mike Payne, Tim Polzer, Reed Poole, Will Pry, Fred Reed III,
Susan Sainz, Evan Salituro, Gary Santaniello, Judi Smalling, Doug Williams, Steve Wilson and Mark Zeske.

Additionally, the Publisher would like to acknowledge the entire staff of Beckett Publications, which was instrumental in the completion of this book: Dana Alecknavage,
Jeff Amano, Jeff Anthony, Kelly Atkins, Claire Backus, Kaye Ball, Airey Baringer, Randy Barning, Eric Best, Julie Binion, Louise Bird, Pat Blandford, Marco Brizuela, Bob Brown,
Chris Calandro, Randall Calvert, Mary Campana, Susan Catka, Jud Chappell, Albert Chavez, Theo Chen, Marty Click, Gary Coleman, Andres Costilla, Lauren Drewes, Ben Ecklar,
Denise Ellison, Craig Ferris, Gean Paul Figari, Jeany Finch, Carol Fowler, Joe Galindo, Gayle Gasperin, Stephen Genusa, Loretta Gibbs, Marcelo Gomes de Souza,
Rosanna Gonzalez-Olaechea, Duane Green, Jeff Greer, Mary Gregory, Robert Gregory, Jenifer Grellhesl, Julie Grove, Patti Harris, Mark Hartley, Mark Harwell, Beth Harwell,
Pepper Hastings, Joanna Hayden, Chris Hellem, Melissa Herzog, Dan Hitt, Mike Jaspersen, Jay Johnson, Steven Judd, Eddie Kelly, Wendy Kizer, Rich Klein, Brian Kosley, Tom Layberger,
Jane Ann Layton, Stanley Lira, Kirk Lockhart, John Marshall, Teri McGahey, Omar Mediano, Beverly Mills, Sherry Monday, Mila Morante, Mike Moss, Allan Muir, Hugh Murphy,
Shawn Murphy, Mike Obert, Stacy Olivieri, Wendy Pallugna, Laura Patterson, Gabriel Rangel, Bob Richardson, Tina Riojas, Grant Sandground, David Schneider, Christine Seibert,
Brett Setter, Dave Sliepka, Sheri Smith, Rob Springs, Margaret Steele, Marcia Stoesz, Phaedra Strecher, Dawn Sturgeon, Doree Tate and Jim Tereschuk.

Foreword

Worth Every Penny

The no-look assist is a Hardaway trademark. And Penny's not a shabby basketball player, either.

NOREN TROTMAN / NBA PHOTOS

Magical Penny Hardaway truly lives up to his status as a role model both on and off the court.

Remember that Nike commercial with Charles Barkley? You know, the one that started all that "I am not a role model!" stuff.

It's true, of course, that Barkley and many other pro athletes shouldn't be expected to play that difficult role. But apparently, Penny Hardaway missed that particular spot. He probably was busy practicing his jump shot or working on his cross-over dribble, or maybe he was in the middle of a hectic Memphis street helping out a stranger.

Ron Higgins, author of our in-depth feature about Penny's off-the-court life (*"Twice As Nice" on page 38*), tells the story:

Penny is driving down Poplar Avenue in downtown Memphis. He sees a woman with four children stranded in the middle lane after their car stalled. So being the assist artist that he is, Penny stops traffic, phones in a distress call to the authorities and gives the woman enough money to buy her and her children a nice dinner.

There were no cameras, tape recorders or notebooks to document the scene. It was simply Penny being Penny. On or off the court, Hardaway lives to hand out the perfect assist.

Of course, this season, with Shaquille O'Neal now in Hollywood, Penny must step up his scoring. Few believe that will be a problem. Just don't ask him to cut down his assist average away from the crowds. After all, role models like Penny have a lot of damage to repair.

Rudy J. Klancnik
Managing Editor

CONTENTS

Front Cover Photo by Rocky Widner
Special Thanks to NBA Photos for its photo contributions.

Flippin' for Li'l Penny
To see Li'l Penny take flight, grasp the pages between thumb and forefinger, keep your eye on the lower right-hand corner, and let 'em flip.

GREG FOSTER / NBA PHOTOS

The Perfectionist

By Tim Povtak

Penny Hardaway's success in basketball and in life lies in his relentless pursuit of perfection

For a week after he and his teammates were swept out of the 1996 NBA playoffs, Anfernee Hardaway went sleepless in Orlando. He agonized over his team's embarrassing collapse in the conference final against the Chicago Bulls.

He searched for answers, but he found none.

He tossed and turned each night, jolted awake by a nightmare — the nightmare that had been a reality. The Orlando Magic had been swept like dirt off the floor, and he felt responsible. He buried his head in the pillow, wondering what more he should have done, could have done; wondering what had gone so dramatically wrong.

Then suddenly, it all became so crystal clear. Anfernee realized it was nothing he couldn't solve the way he always does — by demanding more of himself. He looked in the mirror, and he no longer wanted to be one of the best young players in basketball.

He knew it was time — time to be the best player. And he has slept well ever since. The fear of failure still haunts him. But the pursuit of perfection is what drives him now. It's the battle he wages every day of his life.

It's the balancing act that defines Penny Hardaway — on court and off. It often consumes him, dictating to him. He wants to play the perfect game, build the perfect house, drive the perfect car, dress the perfect way. He plans the work, then works the plan. Anything that diverts him, annoys him. No one works harder. He expects no one to be better.

The pursuit is what makes him a great basketball player, yet it frustrates him endlessly. It is both a blessing and a burden. It can be exhilarating at times, yet exhausting to carry that load. Perfection is the carrot that guides his game and his life. Failure is what he fears most.

So much already has been achieved. So much more is expected.

Hardaway enters the 1996-97 NBA season as the do-everything point guard and unquestioned leader of the Magic, a team now at the crossroads. He already is known as the best point guard in basketball. Back-to-back All-NBA first-team honors provide proof. But that isn't good enough anymore.

The departure of center Shaquille O'Neal dictates that instead of just leading this team, he must carry it. Penny has no choice but to take his game to another level for the Magic to succeed. It's a level few athletes ever visit. A step back for the Magic will be disappointing in his eyes. O'Neal has left, but Hardaway's desire for a championship has not.

"Everyone kept saying our time would come, to just be patient and wait your turn," Hardaway says. "But I'm tired of waiting. I've established myself personally. Now it's time to start winning big. Until you win a championship, you haven't won anything."

Going into his fourth NBA season, Hardaway already had surpassed O'Neal as the one Magic player opponents feared most. But that came as no surprise. There is no phase of the game in which Hardaway doesn't excel. He can score from inside or out. He handles the ball deftly, passes exceptionally, can rebound and defend.

Penny already has proven himself up to the task of carrying the Shaq-less Magic on his shoulders. He guided Orlando through the first six weeks of the '95-96 season with O'Neal sidelined with a fractured thumb, cementing his status as one of the league's best. The Magic posted the best record in the

Penny's latest drive to an NBA title was cut off by the Bulls during the conference finals.

league at 13-4 during that November when Shaq was out. And Hardaway earned NBA Player of the Month honors, averaging 27 points, 6.5 assists and 5.8 rebounds.

Now he must maintain that exceptional play for an entire season.

"I can see my role changing, and everyone piggy-backing onto me," Hardaway said after O'Neal signed with the Lakers. "Wherever the team needs me, that's what I'll do. That's always been my attitude, but now it becomes more important than ever.

"I don't want to be one of the best anymore. I want to be the best player in basketball. At least that's what I strive for," he says. "You know how people say that Michael Jordan is the best to ever play the game. Well, when it's all over, I want them to say that about me. That's how hard I work at it."

He has studied Jordan, and Magic Johnson and Larry Bird — maybe the game's three greatest players — and tried to combine their skills into one perfect player. It may take years to achieve, but he's just 24, merely a babe in his development. He is overflowing with the desire to turn that dream of perfection into reality.

"I don't think anyone in basketball has ever played the perfect game, but it's out there somewhere," Hardaway says. "I know even if I had a game where I made 10 of 10 free throws, 20 of 20 field goals, got 10 assists, a triple double and made no turnovers, it wouldn't be perfect yet. There would always be something I'd miss. That's just the way I think.

"I'm a perfectionist," he admits. "There is no getting around that. And that's why I've always been my own worst critic. A lot of times it gets me into

Penny's quest for perfection continued during his gold-medal run with the U.S. Olympic team.

Penny Earned

A penny saved may be a penny earned, but for Orlando superguard Penny Hardaway, simple basketball deeds are worth much more. Following is a breakdown of how many pennies Penny earned per statistical category in the 1995-96 season, based on his $5,230,000 salary.

Category	Total	Pennies per
Points	1,780	293,820
Assists	582	898,625
Rebounds	354	1,477,401
Field goals	623	839,486
Three-pointers	89	5,876,404

trouble. I shouldn't get so down on myself. But I was taught at an early age to do your best at everything. And don't settle for anything less."

It is a pursuit only a select few ever really understand. Perfection is out there waiting, calling his name in a sensuous tone no one else hears, a sweet song he can't escape. It lures him every time, like a ship to the rocks.

Sometimes, it drives him crazy. Yet it drives him to success after success in his life. Mistakes infuriate him. Erasing them from his memory is difficult.

From video games to free-throw shooting drills, Anfernee Hardaway must win to be satisfied. Playing spades on the team plane is no different. If it's worth the time to do, it's worth the effort to do it well. He dislikes doing interviews, will go to extremes to avoid them, but he has learned how to do them expertly.

His biggest task, as his game develops and the team changes, will be learning to tolerate the weaknesses of others, along with his own mistakes. When he brings the ball upcourt for the Magic, he knows where everyone should be, and what they should be

doing. When a play doesn't develop properly, he wants to know why. He wants to know where it broke down. He wants to know why the Magic can't win every game, why he can't make every shot.

"Everyone on this level is competitive," says teammate Donald Royal. "But he's above the rest of us. He takes every day as a challenge. Even a little pickup game at practice, he hates to lose. He really takes it to heart. That's his edge. That's what makes him stand out from the rest."

Magic head coach Brian Hill has handed the controls of the team to Hardaway. Down the stretch of each game, it is his now to win or lose with the ball in his hands.

"He's a great competitor who absolutely hates losing," Hill says. "He just does the things now that only the great ones can do. That's why you want him controlling the game. He already has done it

time and time again for us."

In the first six weeks last season without O'Neal, he scored the winning basket in the final three seconds three times. He scored with 1.2 seconds remaining to beat Miami, 94-93. He hit a six-foot bank shot at the buzzer to beat Vancouver, 95-93. And he hit an 11-foot jumper with three seconds left to beat Houston, 92-90.

"As the point guard, everything we do starts with me at both ends of the floor. That's why I take the responsibility if things don't go right," Penny says. "I have earned the respect of everyone on this team. I think they respect me now. And they will follow me."

He is not a leader who demands respect. He commands it. He doesn't holler, but his teammates understand how he works. They can tell by the look in his eyes, his expression, his body language. They know what he wants. No one questions him anymore.

In the past, Hardaway was hesitant of being too vocal as a leader, hoping that his teammates would follow his example and his style of play. But now he plans to speak out more, demand more from himself and his teammates.

"You can read it in his face without him saying a word," says Magic assistant coach Tree Rollins. "If someone isn't where he should be, Penny is going to want to know why. And he's going to let that person know. He wants everything exactly right. And he doesn't always understand how it can go wrong."

He is the same way about his game-day routine. His ankles must be taped perfectly, or he wants them taped again. He wants new socks, new wrist bands, for every game. Unlike his teammates, he doesn't wear his game shorts during

By Year Two of his pro career, Penny already found himself in the spotlight of the NBA Finals.

warmups before games. He wears a different pair, then changes just before game time. There is a routine he follows, and he never deviates.

"To me, the most amazing thing is when he dresses casually. Everything always matches perfectly — hats, shoes, shirts, socks, even when he's dressed down," says Magic equipment manager, Rodney Powell. "I'd hate to see his closet at home."

That closet at home soon will change dramatically. Hardaway spent more than $1 million buying up a group of lots in Central Florida's ritziest neighborhood to build his dream home. He talked personally with several builders, architects, craftsmen, designers, trying to make sure the house would be exactly what he wanted before construction began. The plans were drawn up, torn up, redone, revamped and redrawn many times before they met his approval.

When finished, the house will include an indoor gymnasium, a huge game room, a movie room, trophy case room — everything his heart desires, the most perfect house he can imagine.

"I wanted to watch my home go up from the first brick to the last," he says. "I wanted to make it as perfect as I can. A man's home is his castle, and that's what I'll want mine to be. But you know what? I'll have everything I could possible imagine in that home when it's done, and it won't be perfect. The next week, I'll think of something else I should have had put in."

It will be just like his game, but it really will have nothing to do with the millions he earns playing basketball. It was the same way when he was

Perfect Timing

When the clock's running down and the score is close, the Orlando Magic want the basketball in Penny Hardaway's hands. During the 1995-96 season Hardaway consistently came through with game-winning performances in the clutch. The breakdown of Penny's magic:

DATE COMMENTS	OPPONENT	FINAL SCORE
Nov. 8 Scores six of career-high 42 points in third overtime	New Jersey	130-122 (3OT)
Nov. 11 Hits game-winning layup with 1.2 seconds remaining	Miami	94-93
Nov. 14 Hits a key three-pointer with 1:07 to play	Chicago	94-88
Nov. 22 Banks in game-winning shot at the buzzer	Vancouver	95-93
Nov. 25 Scores 13 of his 30 points in fourth quarter	Washington	114-112
Dec. 6 Swishes two free throws with 22.2 seconds to play	Golden State	109-107
Dec. 25 Hits an 11-foot jumper with 3.1 seconds remaining	Houston	92-90
Jan. 30 Completes a three-point play with 18 seconds remaining	Boston	104-99

DATE COMMENTS	OPPONENT	FINAL SCORE
March 8 Grabs key rebound at end of regulation	Charlotte	117-112 (OT)
March 15 Scores five of game-high 29 points in overtime	Vancouver	92-87 (OT)
March 22 Scores five of his 30 points in final 1:50 of overtime	Washington	111-108 (OT)
April 21 Scores 11 of his 19 points in final 4:11 of the game	Charlotte	103-100

BARRY GOSSAGE / NBA PHOTOS

Penny's like money in the bank.

growing up with no money in his pocket. He was raised by his grandmother in a tiny, one bedroom house on the poor side of Memphis. He was poor, but he

As the Shaq-less era begins, Penny quietly assumes the role of the Magic's No. 1 player.

was perfectly poor.

"I think it all started with my grandmother and the way she raised me," he says. "She used to make me get up at 6 a.m., even when we didn't have school. It was a routine. We always had to clean the room, do the chores and eat breakfast before we could do any-

thing else. Everything had to be done just so. Everything had to be done just perfectly." •

Tim Povtak covers the Magic for The Orlando Sentinel.

Say What?

From his friendship with Penny Hardaway to his impending acting career, Li'l Penny tells all

Li'l Penny,

short as he is, has been a marketing giant for Nike through the last couple of years. His outlandish personality and his quick-wit humor have brought him to the forefront of popularity. Since he began appearing in television commercials with his buddy, Orlando Magic guard Penny Hardaway, Nike's campaign for the Air Penny shoes has skyrocketed.

Despite his hectic schedule, Li'l Penny recently found time to sit down

Caught on tape: Penny and his sidekick star in a new batch of Nike spots this season.

with Beckett Publications assistant editor Mike Pagel for an exclusive one-on-one interview. As expected, Li'l Penny was his outspoken self.

Mike Pagel: Are you a mentor to Penny Hardaway, a friend or are you just another part of his posse?

Li'l Penny: **I am all three really. But I'm Penny's friend first and foremost. Penny and I have been through a lot together, and in a world where he meets all kinds of people who are always wanting something from him, he knows that I have been with him since the early days, and he is my friend. As far as being a mentor, well, I don't know about that. But I have taught him a few things. Like just last week, I taught him how to make**

Unlike his hoops game, Li'l Penny's storytelling skills can capture anyone's attention.

Bananas Foster. Have you ever had it? It's delicious.

MP: Penny Hardaway starred in the movie, *Blue Chips*. How would you say your new acting career is coming along?

LP: Well, I'm entertaining offers. There's been talk of a remake of *The Fish that Saved Pittsburgh* that I am interested in, and I was supposed to play the Will Smith role in *Independence Day*, but I demanded major rewrites and butted heads with the studio brass, so that fell through.

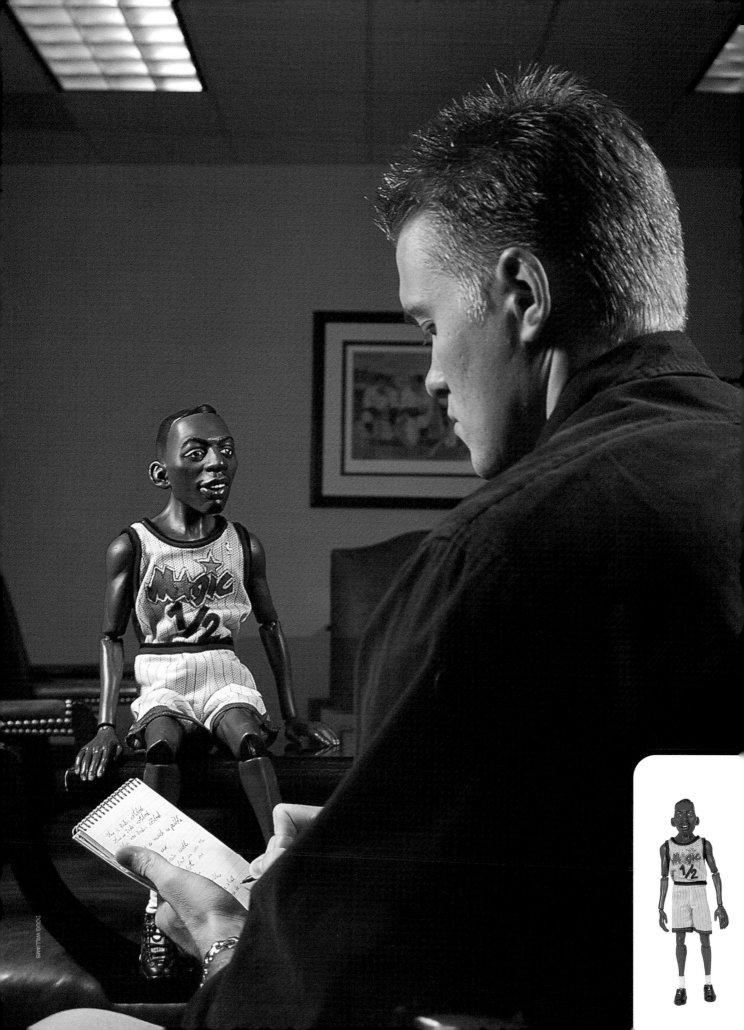

DOUG WILLIAMS

MP: Did Shaquille O'Neal consult with you before making his decision to sign with the Lakers?

LP: No, man. I try to stay out of all that contract stuff. But if he had consulted with me, I would have told him to stay in Orlando and play with Penny. They would have been the Kareem and Magic [combo] of today's game, but I guess he wanted the L.A. life. I wish him well, but he'll be shaking his head when Penny leads the Magic to a championship.

MP: Be honest now, who do you think has a better move to the hole, you or Penny?

LP: No question. Penny. He has the best move to the hole of anyone on the planet. I encourage him to be more aggressive out there, and this season, with the court opened up, you'll see, Penny is going to take his game to a whole 'nother level.

MP: You trashed Penny's house, you've embarrassed him in front of supermodel Tyra Banks and you caused him to turn the ball over in a game against the Knicks. Why does Penny put up with you?

LP: Because we're best friends. I mean come on, no one gets on your nerves like your best

Li'l Penny reels off another in his line of fish stories. He later proved his vertical leap was not quite that high.

friend. But no one makes you laugh or helps you out like your best friend either, so it's give and take. Plus, Penny does plenty to bug me, but you never see that in the Nike spots. They should do a Nike commercial about how loud Penny likes to watch the television, or how he puts ketchup on everything, or how when we were little kids he put me in a clothes dryer. How about a commercial about those things?   •

Mike Pagel is an assistant editor at Beckett Publications.

A Li'l Hobby

It seems Li'l Penny is quite a basketball card-collecting junkie. In his own words, here are his favorite Penny Hardaway cards.

• 1995-96 Upper Deck #316 — "Atlanta was an experience. I traded pins like nobody's business. That Varsity Restaurant pin with the onion rings as the Olympic rings? I have 12. Anyway, this card will always remind me of Penny's work-shaking gold medal performance in '96, and I well up with pride every time I look at it."

• 1994-95 Hoops #264 — "Look how young Penny looks on this card. Rookie Game MVP. He put on a show in that game. Unfortunately, the trophy he's holding was on display in our recreation room until it was shattered during a party I threw while Penny was on the road. Sometimes when I'm dancing, and I've got the feeling, I get a little sloppy."

• 1993-94 Stadium Club #308 — "Check out the look on my man wearing #50. And look at everyone else in this card, just standing around, watching Penny finish. You can't stop Penny, you can only hope to not be caught in a card looking silly."

• 1994-95 Stadium Club #17 — "Which brings me to this card, which proves that the Phoenix Suns understand that it's better to let Penny have his two than to be caught in the card looking silly. There's not a Sun in sight. It's just Penny, all alone, finishing."

• 1995-96 Stadium Club #32 — "I like this card, because it looks like Penny's just flying, knifing, through the lane. And, he's getting ready to release a smooth finger roll in honor of one of our favorite players, George Gervin. This is also the official card of the Greg Dreiling School of Pressure Defense."

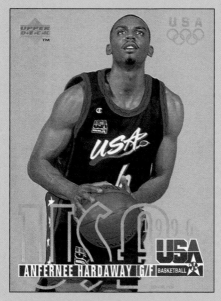

1995-96 Upper Deck #316

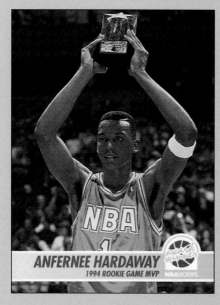

1994-95 Hoops #264

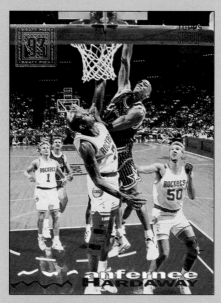

1993-94 Stadium Club #308

1994-95 Stadium Club #17

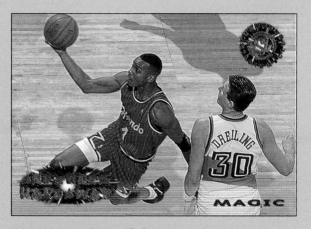

1995-96 Stadium Club #32

HEART

By Brian Schmitz

GOLD

OF

Distraught over a deadly bomb explosion and Shaquille O'Neal's departure, Hardaway grew up during his Olympic experience

The United States' gold-medal victory in men's basketball during the Summer Olympics was a foregone conclusion, a mere coronation staged by the NBA's biggest superstars.

Formality or not, team member Anfernee Hardaway needed the feel-good experience to help chase away the summer blues.

"This means a lot to me," said Hardaway, admiring his gold medal. "I'm going to put this up on my wall so I can see it every day."

Even though he knew the Dream Team would roll, Hardaway enjoyed the happy ending perhaps more than most. It was his first championship of any kind — "since I played on an AAU team in Memphis," he says, and maybe his last for a long while.

For Penny, it had been an Olympics to remember and an Olympics to forget.

A day before Opening Ceremonies, he was blindsided by the shocking news that his Orlando Magic teammate, Shaquille O'Neal, was no longer his Orlando Magic teammate.

Then, midway through the Games, a pipe bomb exploded outside the team hotel in Centennial Olympic Park, an unsettling, sobering experience to say the least. Olympic officials tightened security even more around the Dream Team, and Hardaway elected to avoid crowds and stay at the hotel.

He didn't feel much like mingling anyway. O'Neal, a free agent, had signed a $120 million, seven-year contract to play for the Los Angeles Lakers on Thursday, July 18 — Hardaway's birthday, of all days.

"We had a party Friday night, but I wasn't into it . . . that's probably the worst birthday that I ever had because I heard he was going to L.A. and then they had the press conference.

"I think the first day I was kind of devastated," Hardaway says. "I wasn't saying a lot and the guys [Dream Team teammates] saw changes in my attitude. I was kind of hurt, but I got over it and said we just have to go on.

"You lose a player like Shaquille, you can't be happy the remainder of the Olympics. It's always going to put a damper on it whether we win a gold medal or not because going into the regular season, we're [the Magic] not going to be full strength."

Hardaway and O'Neal had been teammates in Orlando for three seasons, winning an Eastern Conference title and appearing in the NBA Finals against the Houston Rockets. They were the backbone of a team many considered a future dynasty. What bothered Penny was that Shaq never hinted he was leaving during two weeks of practices and exhibitions leading up the Olympics.

"I got a call. I can't say from whom, but it was about seven in the morning and they told me that Shaquille had signed with the Lakers at 3 a.m. It all came together because Shaquille wasn't with us [the Dream Team] when we were getting our gear," Hardaway says. "When everybody got on the bus, he wasn't there. I suspected something was up."

Hardaway greeted many of his undersized and overmatched opponents with powerful performances, including 15 points and 10 assists against China.

Hardaway admitted it was awkward being around O'Neal after he signed. "You have guys joking with you, saying, 'you're going to be in the lottery now' . . . that's what was so tough."

Hardaway tried to squash rumors of a rift between the two young superstars in Orlando. "I've talked about it with Shaquille," he says. "I don't think Shaquille's gripe is with me. It's with the management. Who knows what happened, but he's gone now and I wish him the best.

"We had a two-minute conversation. . . . I didn't ask him what happened. I didn't ask anything because I was still in shock. My gut feeling was that he was going to stay. I cannot be selfish. Shaquille has to do what he has to do. It's a business. Evidently he felt more comfortable out in L.A. I think he loves L.A. as a city. I think he found his dream."

Penny had found his dream, too, representing his country and joining the NBA's most elite circle. He had scrimmaged against the original Dream Team in '92 as a member of a college select squad.

"I think that this is on the top of my list as far as all the accomplishments," he says. "This is No. 1 because you're playing for your country and to go in the gym and hear all the people chanting 'U.S.A.' makes you feel great."

Hardaway, admitted he had to put Shaq's signing behind him in Olympic play or "I would not only be cheating myself, but I would be cheating my country if I wasn't playing as hard as I can, instead of worrying about what's going to happen with the Magic."

And play hard he did. Hardaway averaged 10.2 points and five assists per game as the United States crushed all eight of its opponents en route to winning the gold medal.

Penny chipped in with 14 points in the team's 98-75 quarterfinal victory over Brazil. He added 14 more in the 101-73 semifinal rout of Australia.

But it was in the finale, a 95-69 victory over Yugoslavia, that Hardaway showcased his all-around skills for the world. He keyed a first-half run with a three-pointer, a steal and a jumper that gave the sluggish Americans a seven-point lead near halftime. Then he made several highlight-film assists to David Robinson. Penny's repertoire included an acrobatic dunk that brought out the loudest cheers of the night.

"I wanted it very badly," he says. "This was my first time around. Ever since I practiced against the first Dream Team I had dreams of being on an Olympic team."

The gold medal helped erase some unsettling memories. On Saturday, July 27, around 1:15 a.m., Hardaway expe-

Hardaway enjoyed mingling and trading autographs with his USA Olympic teammates, including gymnast, Dominique Dawes.

rienced something that put life and sports in perspective. A pipe-bomb exploded in Centennial Olympic Park, killing one person and injuring 111 others.

"It made me mad because you can't continue to live your life afraid, thinking something is going to happen every other minute," Penny says. "I was actually awake [when the bomb exploded]. I thought it was thunder because I was on the inside of the hotel and all the rooms [facing] the street where the bomb blew up could hear it easily. Security called and said a bomb went off and to go downstairs. They didn't have to finish the conversation."

For Hardaway, the Olympics were never quite the same after that.

"It took away from the women's gymnastics and what had just happened with Kerri Strug. It took away from all the gold medals won by us, really, just tainted it a little bit. You were looking at something [the Olympics] where all nationalities can get along and be

together, but it all came to a halt over a bomb," he says.

"It's a scary feeling. Once you learn about what happened you just feel so sorry about the families and friends of the people who died and the people who were injured . . . just helpless people, innocent people."

Shy and introverted by nature, Hardaway seldom ventured away from the team hotel.

"The older guys told me that one negative about the Olympics being in America was not being able to go anywhere," he says. "I just planted myself in the hotel. It's like 'the rock', you know the movie — *The Rock*. You just can't get out."

Penny passed the time at the hotel playing Ping-Pong with Reggie Miller, shooting pool and playing video games. He watched the women's gymnastics and Michael Johnson sprint to glory.

After the Olympics, Hardaway recognized another mission: Becoming Orlando's unquestioned floor leader.

The gold-medal winning performance against Yugoslavia secured Penny's first gold medal and his first team championship of any kind.

And for him, associating with veterans such as Robinson, Charles Barkley and other Dream Teamers, served as his preseason, at least mentally.

"When you're with guys like Charles [Barkley] and Karl [Malone] and John [Stockton] and David [Robinson], you watch them, you see how they do things, what they say in the huddles," Hardaway says. "And I'm going to take all that back to Orlando."

Without Shaq, he'll need everything he can get.   •

Brian Schmitz covered the '96 Summer Olympics for The Orlando Sentinel.

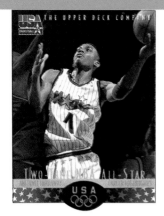

Game No. 2

Dream Team 87, Angola 54
July 22, Georgia Dome, Atlanta

Angola

Player	Min	FG	FGA	FT	FTA	REB	AST	PTS
Anibal Moreira	26	0	4	2	2	1	3	2
Angelo Victoriano	22	3	9	0	0	2	1	8
Benjamin Ucuahamba	27	1	5	0	0	1	5	2
Antonio Carvalho	29	6	11	0	0	4	1	16
David Dias	31	3	10	2	2	5	0	10
Edmar Victoriano	16	0	2	4	4	0	2	4
Herlander Coimbra	8	0	1	0	0	1	0	0
Justino Victoriano	27	3	5	0	0	1	0	6
Benjamin Romano	11	2	4	0	0	1	0	6
Jose Guimares	5	0	1	0	0	1	0	0
Totals	**200**	**18**	**52**	**8**	**8**	**17**	**12**	**54**

Dream Team

Player	Min	FG	FGA	FT	FTA	REB	AST	PTS
Grant Hill	20	2	3	2	3	6	3	7
Penny Hardaway	17	1	3	0	1	2	2	2
Mitch Richmond	19	4	8	0	0	1	2	10
Karl Malone	22	6	11	0	0	6	0	12
Shaquille O'Neal	20	3	7	1	3	3	1	7
Charles Barkley	18	3	3	1	2	9	7	7
David Robinson	10	2	4	0	0	1	0	4
Scottie Pippen	20	5	9	1	2	2	3	11
Reggie Miller	21	4	6	0	0	2	0	10
John Stockton	9	2	2	2	2	1	2	7
Gary Payton	14	3	5	2	3	2	3	8
Hakeem Olajuwon	10	0	0	2	2	2	1	2
Totals	**200**	**35**	**61**	**12**	**18**	**37**	**24**	**87**

"Shaquille and all of them are going to get their dunks and get the crowd going, but we've just got to get up by 20 or 30 before we start acting crazy and doing all this fancy stuff." — Gary Payton

Game No. 1

Dream Team 96, Argentina 68
July 20, Georgia Dome, Atlanta

Argentina

Player	Min	FG	FGA	FT	FTA	REB	AST	PTS
Marcelo Nicola	30	4	9	3	4	4	3	13
Diego Osella	15	0	1	1	4	0	1	1
Ruben Wolkowisky	28	2	6	5	10	2	1	9
Juan Espil	33	7	15	10	11	2	0	27
Marcelo Milanesio	36	2	5	3	3	2	7	8
Daniel Farabello	5	0	0	0	0	0	0	0
Luis Villar	4	0	0	0	0	0	0	0
Ernesto Michel	3	1	1	0	0	1	0	2
Fabricio Oberto	10	0	1	0	0	3	0	0
Jorge Racca	27	2	4	1	2	3	2	6
Esteban Perez	10	1	3	0	0	0	0	2
Totals	**200**	**19**	**45**	**23**	**34**	**17**	**14**	**68**

Dream Team

Player	Min	FG	FGA	FT	FTA	REB	AST	PTS
Charles Barkley	15	4	5	1	2	4	0	9
Scottie Pippen	23	3	7	2	2	4	2	8
David Robinson	17	5	7	8	10	7	0	18
Reggie Miller	22	2	5	2	2	2	2	6
John Stockton	12	2	3	2	2	0	3	6
Grant Hill	25	5	7	0	0	4	5	10
Penny Hardaway	23	1	3	2	2	5	5	4
Mitch Richmond	23	2	4	4	4	1	1	9
Karl Malone	10	2	4	1	2	2	0	5
Shaquille O'Neal	13	6	8	1	3	4	0	13
Gary Payton	10	1	4	0	2	3	2	2
Hakeem Olajuwon	7	3	5	0	0	1	0	6
Totals	**200**	**36**	**62**	**23**	**30**	**37**	**20**	**96**

"We played to their tempo. We got into foul trouble early, and they were always at the free-throw line." — Penny Hardaway

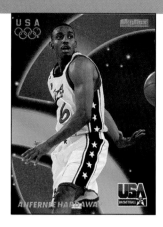

Game No. 4

Dream Team 133, China 70
July 26, Georgia Dome, Atlanta

Dream Team

Player	Min	FG	FGA	FT	FTA	REB	AST	PTS
Scottie Pippen	17	10	14	0	0	2	4	24
Reggie Miller	18	6	9	0	0	1	1	17
Karl Malone	23	5	7	1	2	6	3	11
Shaquille O'Neal	21	5	8	3	3	10	3	13
Gary Payton	14	0	0	0	0	2	9	0
Grant Hill	23	6	9	6	7	4	5	19
Penny Hardaway	21	6	8	3	3	1	10	15
David Robinson	7	4	4	0	0	3	0	8
Mitch Richmond	22	5	12	2	2	0	2	14
John Stockton	15	2	4	1	1	1	2	5
Hakeem Olajuwon	15	3	6	1	2	5	2	7
Totals	**200**	**52**	**81**	**17**	**20**	**35**	**41**	**133**

China

Player	Min	FG	FGA	FT	FTA	REB	AST	PTS
Li Xiaoyong	31	1	4	0	0	3	5	2
Zheng Wu	20	2	5	0	0	1	1	5
Sun Jun	26	3	5	0	0	3	4	7
Liu Yudong	27	7	14	4	7	5	2	18
Menk Batere	22	3	6	0	0	6	1	6
Wang Zhizhi	25	3	7	0	0	3	1	6
Hu Weidong	20	6	9	0	0	3	3	15
Wu Naiquin	6	0	0	0	0	0	0	0
Li Nan	14	2	6	0	0	3	1	4
Totals	**200**	**29**	**60**	**5**	**9**	**27**	**18**	**70**

"This was the first time the team has played well, and it was a welcome relief." — Charles Barkley

Game No. 3

Dream Team 104, Lithuania 84
July 24, Georgia Dome, Atlanta

Lithuania

Player	Min	FG	FGA	FT	FTA	REB	AST	PTS
Rytis Vaisvila	10	3	5	0	0	1	1	7
Saulius Stombergas	10	1	4	2	2	1	1	5
Rimas Kurtinaitis	8	2	5	3	3	1	2	8
Arvydas Sabonis	5	2	6	0	0	2	1	6
Gintaras Einikis	18	8	15	5	5	7	2	21
Mindaugas Zukauskas	5	0	2	0	0	0	0	0
Eurelijus Zukauskas	11	0	2	0	0	6	0	0
Tomas Pacesas	10	2	3	0	0	3	5	5
Darius Lukminas	12	6	8	0	0	0	1	15
Arturas Karnisovas	10	4	7	6	8	7	4	15
Totals	**200**	**28**	**57**	**16**	**18**	**28**	**16**	**82**

Dream Team

Player	Min	FG	FGA	FT	FTA	REB	AST	PTS
Charles Barkley	8	4	6	8	12	5	3	16
Scottie Pippen	13	6	9	1	5	4	1	13
Reggie Miller	10	5	11	1	1	1	2	14
Gary Payton	10	2	2	2	2	3	4	8
Hakeem Olajuwon	7	1	4	0	0	3	3	2
Grant Hill	10	3	5	2	4	2	3	9
Penny Hardaway	NA	2	3	1	2	2	3	6
David Robinson	9	2	5	2	3	2	0	6
Mitch Richmond	10	2	6	1	4	3	1	7
Karl Malone	12	5	7	4	4	3	2	14
John Stockton	10	1	2	1	2	2	4	3
Shaquille O'Neal	NA	3	6	0	1	3	2	6
Totals	**200**	**36**	**66**	**23**	**40**	**33**	**28**	**104**

"They were really hurting without Sarunas [Marciulionis], because that's when the backup guard has to come in and start and play a role that he's not used to playing." — Penny Hardaway

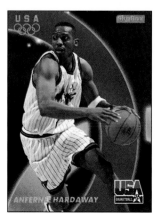

Game No. 5

Dream Team 102, Croatia 71

July 28, Georgia Dome, Atlanta

Croatia

Player	Min	FG	FGA	FT	FTA	REB	AST	PTS
Toni Kukoc	33	4	11	0	0	3	10	10
Vladan Alanovic	27	1	5	0	0	2	2	2
Slaven Rimac	19	4	5	3	4	1	0	14
Stojan Vrankovic	12	1	2	0	0	2	1	2
Dino Radja	35	4	11	1	2	4	0	9
Josip Vrankovic	12	2	3	0	0	1	1	6
Velimir Perasovic	20	0	2	0	0	1	0	0
Zan Tabak	23	8	13	3	4	7	0	19
Damir Mulaomeric	13	2	4	2	4	2	3	7
Davor Marcelic	14	1	2	0	0	0	1	2
Totals	**200**	**27**	**58**	**9**	**14**	**23**	**18**	**71**

Dream Team

Player	Min	FG	FGA	FT	FTA	REB	AST	PTS
Charles Barkley	24	7	9	0	0	12	1	14
David Robinson	15	4	5	5	9	3	0	13
Scottie Pippen	19	3	9	0	0	1	3	9
Mitch Richmond	25	5	8	5	5	5	3	16
Gary Payton	22	2	5	3	4	4	7	8
Grant Hill	21	4	6	1	2	0	2	9
Penny Hardaway	13	0	5	0	0	4	6	0
Reggie Miller	15	3	7	0	0	0	3	7
Karl Malone	16	4	5	2	4	3	1	10
John Stockton	9	1	2	0	0	2	2	2
Shaquille O'Neal	12	3	5	2	4	3	0	8
Hakeem Olajuwon	13	3	6	0	0	4	1	6
Totals	**200**	**39**	**72**	**18**	**28**	**41**	**29**	**102**

"We're building. We're coming together. The last two games, we came out right." — Mitch Richmond

Quarterfinal

Dream Team 98, Brazil 75

July 30, Georgia Dome, Atlanta

Brazil

Player	Min	FG	FGA	FT	FTA	REB	AST	PTS
Andre Fonseca	17	1	4	0	0	3	3	2
Joao Jose Vianna	27	2	6	2	2	4	0	6
Wilson Fernando Minuci	30	5	8	1	2	4	5	11
Oscar Schmidt	31	8	20	6	6	5	2	26
Joelcio Joerke	31	2	6	1	8	10	1	5
Demetrius Ferraciu	3	0	3	0	0	1	0	0
Caio Cassiolato	20	6	12	0	0	0	3	14
Olivia Do Nascimento	11	2	7	0	0	5	1	5
Caio Franco Silveira	7	1	4	1	2	2	1	3
Antonio Jose Santana	4	0	0	0	0	1	0	0
Rogerio Klafke	20	1	3	0	0	0	1	3
Totals	**200**	**28**	**73**	**11**	**20**	**35**	**17**	**75**

Dream Team

Player	Min	FG	FGA	FT	FTA	REB	AST	PTS
Scottie Pippen	23	6	9	0	0	4	6	13
Reggie Miller	22	5	9	0	0	1	2	12
Karl Malone	21	4	7	1	3	5	2	9
Shaquille O'Neal	21	5	8	1	1	11	0	11
Gary Payton	23	3	6	1	4	5	7	7
Charles Barkley	15	4	6	0	0	2	2	9
Grant Hill	17	2	6	0	0	1	3	4
Penny Hardaway	17	4	4	6	9	2	4	14
David Robinson	9	1	3	3	4	5	0	5
Mitch Richmond	10	2	3	1	1	0	1	7
John Stockton	9	0	1	0	0	0	0	0
Hakeem Olajuwon	13	2	2	3	5	2	1	7
Totals	**200**	**38**	**64**	**16**	**27**	**38**	**28**	**98**

"They came out and played much better compared to the last game we played. But I still think that no matter who we play, when we go to our bench, there's no way they can keep with us." — Scottie Pippen

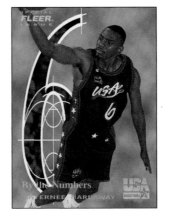

Semifinal

Dream Team 101, Australia 73
August 1, Georgia Dome, Atlanta

Dream Team

Player	Min	FG	FGA	FT	FTA	REB	AST	PTS
Charles Barkley	24	7	7	9	11	11	2	24
David Robinson	22	7	11	0	0	9	0	14
Scottie Pippen	29	2	10	2	2	10	5	6
Mitch Richmond	13	3	8	3	3	2	0	9
Gary Payton	19	2	11	2	4	4	2	6
Penny Hardaway	19	6	19	0	1	3	1	14
Reggie Miller	22	2	6	0	0	0	3	5
Karl Malone	19	3	7	0	0	6	3	6
John Stockton	15	1	4	1	2	0	2	3
Shaquille O'Neal	18	5	7	4	8	8	1	14
Totals	**200**	**38**	**81**	**21**	**31**	**53**	**19**	**101**

Australia

Player	Min	FG	FGA	FT	FTA	REB	AST	PTS
Tony Ronaldson	28	1	6	2	2	1	2	4
Andrew Gaze	38	6	12	10	11	4	3	25
Shane Heal	35	5	11	5	7	4	5	19
Mark Bradtke	29	3	15	3	4	11	0	9
Andrew Vlahov	23	3	8	2	2	3	2	9
Brett Maher	2	0	0	0	0	0	0	0
Scott Fisher	10	0	2	1	2	3	0	1
Pat Reidy	12	1	4	0	0	0	1	2
Sam MacKinnon	6	1	1	0	0	2	0	2
Tonny Jensen	1	0	0	0	0	0	0	0
Ray Borner	4	0	2	2	2	2	0	2
John Dorge	11	0	0	0	0	1	1	0
Totals	**200**	**20**	**61**	**25**	**30**	**31**	**14**	**73**

"It's kind of hard playing international basketball, but being in the NBA and playing with so many great players has really helped me out." — Penny Hardaway

Final

Dream Team 95, Yugoslavia 69
August 3, Georgia Dome, Atlanta

Yugoslavia

Player	Min	FG	FGA	FT	FTA	REB	AST	PTS
Dejan Bodiroga	30	4	7	5	7	5	1	13
Predrag Danilovic	40	2	6	5	10	2	0	9
Zarko Paspalj	32	8	11	2	4	2	0	19
Aleksandr Djordevic	36	4	8	4	5	5	6	13
Vlade Divac	25	0	6	4	6	3	0	4
Sasa Obradovic	15	1	2	3	5	2	0	6
Nikola Loncar	2	0	0	0	0	0	0	0
Zejko Rebraca	18	2	6	0	2	3	3	4
Dejan Tomasevic	1	0	0	1	2	1	0	1
Milenko Topic	1	0	0	0	0	0	0	0
Totals	**200**	**21**	**46**	**24**	**41**	**23**	**10**	**69**

Dream Team

Player	Min	FG	FGA	FT	FTA	REB	AST	PTS
Scottie Pippen	19	2	4	0	0	4	2	4
Reggie Miller	30	6	11	5	6	1	4	20
Karl Malone	10	0	3	0	2	5	0	0
Gary Payton	16	1	4	0	0	2	2	2
Hakeem Olajuwon	13	1	6	3	4	5	0	5
Charles Barkley	14	2	2	4	6	3	2	8
Penny Hardaway	24	5	8	6	7	3	4	17
David Robinson	26	9	11	10	14	7	0	28
Mitch Richmond	24	2	5	0	0	1	0	5
John Stockton	19	1	1	2	2	0	7	4
Shaquille O'Neal	5	1	1	0	0	0	0	2
Totals	**200**	**30**	**56**	**30**	**41**	**31**	**21**	**95**

"This is a dream come true. This is what we have all been waiting for. All the guys stepped up and got the job done tonight. We really hushed up a lot of the critics and won the gold." — Penny Hardaway

GIVE ME THE ROCK

MAGIC SHOW

Penny Hardaway's

dazzling talents

and growing

popularity add up

to a marketing

slam dunk on

Madison Avenue

By Sean Perry

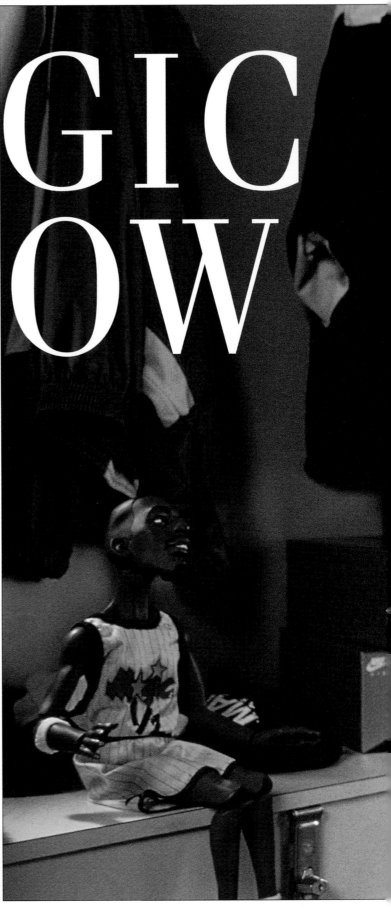

Short in size but long in wind, Li'l Penny has contributed to Hardaway's increasing popularity.

Everyone loves a winner — be it NBA fans or marketing moguls in search of a superstar player to endorse their products.

Penny Hardaway fits that description, and generates the excitement that makes him an appealing character on Madison Avenue.

Why? Consider one particular game during the 1995-96 season: Less than five seconds remain in the game. The Orlando Magic trail intrastate rival Miami by only one point. All that stands between lead Magician Penny Hardaway and a victory is Miami's 250-pound All-Star center, Alonzo Mourning.

In heroic fashion, the slender point guard slips around the perimeter with a crossover dribble and takes it right to the villain.

Exploding to the rim, Hardaway snaps in a layup over 'Zo's head as the buzzer sounds. With a youthful exuberance, he darts off the floor, arms pumping to the crowd.

Following the game he describes his heroic performance by saying, "I took the game on my shoulders, and I just knew I had to get to the basket."

All other comments from Hardaway's mouth either praised the determination of his opponents or the success of his team. This humble and unassuming approach has underscored his dominant presence on the hardwood and has placed him high atop the list of marketable athletes.

Not only is the two-time All-NBA selection considered by teammates a sure thing in a close game, but he also is gaining recognition as a sure thing on Madison Avenue.

Following an impressive sophomore season in which he averaged 25 points per game against the Rockets in the NBA Finals, the promotional opportunities came knocking. NBA Properties named Penny a spokesman and Nike acknowledged him as its second major basketball representative by inking him to a Jordan-like deal. The original Nike big boy agreed that all the fuss was legitimate.

"He's playing with a lot of poise and confidence and that's a great feeling to have," Michael Jordan says. "If I were going to hand the torch to another player, it would be him."

Hardaway may not have to wait for Jordan to step down to dethrone the former fan favorite. Results from a study conducted by Teenage Research Unlimited in the spring of 1996 reveal that Hardaway has surpassed Jordan as the most popular athlete among teenagers. Jordan had held the top spot in the poll for the last eight years. *(Please see chart on page 37.)*

Although Hardaway's numbers have been impressive throughout his career, they still don't seem to justify recognition as the heir to "Air," just yet. Jordan still maintains four championships and four MVPs over the young superstar.

Even after playing second fiddle to the promo-prince Shaquille O'Neal his first three seasons, Hardaway still became the most-beloved Magician by Orlando fans. In polls conducted after his second and third seasons, he received three times as many votes as

As evidenced in this commercial shoot for the NBA, when it comes to show business, Hardaway doesn't clown around.

BARRY GOSSAGE / NBA PHOTOS

Li'l Penny always enjoys watching Hardaway take on an NBA opponent, especially when he's accompanied courtside by supermodel Tyra Banks.

O'Neal. So, what is it that makes this shy sharpshooter so popular?

"If sports has a tarnished image," Erin Patton of Nike says. "Penny's a shining example of what an athlete should be."

Like a clever jazz musician, Hardaway speaks with a quiet confidence and plays with an explosive melody. Yet in contrast, he never 'toots his own horn.' He never seems to have a bad thing to say about anyone.

Enter "Li'l Penny." This obnoxious alter ego puppet does all the talking for the subtle superstar. In his advertisements, "Big Penny" does everything he can to keep the pint-sized, goateed look-a-like from ruining his reputation. Instead of crushing Hardaway's image, however, his boisterous little buddy has produced a giant impact on his marketing potential and the sales of his shoes.

"It's been our best-selling basketball shoe outside of the Air Jordan line ever," Nike public relations director, Tom Feuer says of the "Air Penny" campaign.

This Penny didn't always appear so golden, though. When Nike executives originally questioned Hardaway on a theme for the advertisements, they realized he wasn't the easiest personality to promote. As "Air Jordan" takes to flight and "Sir Charles" drops elbows on Godzilla, Hardaway just seems to be a nice guy, without any other defining characteristics.

Utilizing the sarcastic quips of actor/comedian Chris Rock, Nike added a little flavor to his appeal. In the first episode of "Li'l Penny," he bothers the 6-7 version about passing on a message

RAY AMATI / NBA PHOTOS

Instead of hitting the town following an exhausting NBA game, Penny often plays four more quarters of basketball.

to his former science classmate, Minnesota forward Kevin Garnett. Of course, Hardaway is busy preparing for the game and just blows off his miniature nemesis. The subject of their conversation, the youngest NBA player in the Nike camp, considered the advertisement a compliment.

"Penny's smooth . . . and he's a real great guy," Garnett says. "He's a real swell dude. Somebody for a young guy like myself to try to pattern after — a great role model."

As the younger generation of NBA superstars attempt to mold themselves after the two-time All-Star, the elder statesmen of the league appreciate his mature qualities.

"He doesn't talk," Jazz forward Karl Malone says. "He just plays the game."

Former teammate Greg Kite explains Hardaway's endearing personality, "Of guys I've played with, Larry Bird has the most drive and desire. Anfernee is the closest to him."

Hardaway realizes the importance of being a responsible role model and possibly the future ambassador of the NBA. It has become evident that the points he scores in his street clothes may be as valuable as the ones he throws down in the black and blue uniforms of the Orlando Magic.

"My image is more important than anything," he says. "I want everybody to say positive things about Anfernee Hardaway. I want them to say he's a very nice gentleman."

With more than $70 million at his disposal, and international celebrity status, many 25-year-olds would opt for life in the fast lane. Hardaway is the exception to the rule. He doesn't indulge in the hectic nightlife and after games usually retires to his Orlando mansion for a good game of NBA Jams or a movie, rather than the downtown nightclubs.

"I never really tried drinking and I've never touched a cigarette," he explains. "My morals are better than that."

Cari Coats, director of marketing for the Orlando Magic, cherishes Hardaway as a member of the Magic.

"Obviously, he's a very positive role model," she says. "It is a professional sports team's dream. That's what we have in Penny, and we're very, very fortunate."

With his diverse basketball skills and clever craftsmanship, he has earned the respect of his NBA opponents. Off the court, his disciplined lifestyle and humble manner has brought Hardaway the admiration of the impressionable younger generation.

Now, unquestionably "The Man" in Orlando, Penny has set his on-the-court goals extremely high. When selecting his number as a rookie, he may have seemed somewhat prophetic, considering both his basketball performance and his marketability.

"Because of my nickname, I thought it would be good for endorsements," he says. "I thought I could do a lot of things with the number '1.' "

As long as he leaves the trash talking to Li'l Penny and the sizzling on-court performances to himself, then it's likely Hardaway will continue to live up to the number on the back of his jersey.

"Penny is getting better and better every day," head coach Brian Hill says.

Hardaway seems to agree, "The best is yet to come." •

Sean Perry is the editor of Axis: Orlando Magazine.

NO. 1 IS NO. 1

In a recent nationwide poll conducted by Teenage Research Unlimited, Penny Hardaway rates as the most popular athlete among teenagers. Michael Jordan, who had held the No. 1 ranking for the previous eight years, fell into a tie for second with Detroit Pistons superstar, Grant Hill. Lakers center Shaquille O'Neal, who had climbed as high as No. 2, has tumbled to No. 15. The complete results:

Rank	Athlete	TRU* Score
1.	Penny Hardaway	54
2.	Michael Jordan	53
2.	Grant Hill	53
4.	Jerry Rice	50
4.	Cal Ripken Jr.	50
6.	Emmitt Smith	49
7.	Shawn Kemp	48
7.	Barry Sanders	48
9.	David Robinson	47
9.	Steve Young	47
11.	Frank Thomas	46
12.	Scottie Pippen	45
12.	Dennis Rodman	45
12.	Chris Webber	45
15.	Shaquille O'Neal	44
16.	Ken Griffey Jr.	43
16.	Jason Kidd	43
16.	Alonzo Mourning	43
19.	Reggie Miller	42
20.	Tim Hardaway	40
21.	Jerry Stackhouse	35
22.	Hakeem Olajuwon	34
22.	Jamal Mashburn	34
24.	Mike Tyson	33
25.	Greg Maddux	31
25.	Latrell Sprewell	31
27.	Joe Smith	28
28.	Glenn Robinson	26
29.	Eddie Murray	25
30.	Drew Bledsoe	21
30.	Kevin Garnett	21
30.	Hideo Nomo	21
33.	Cedric Ceballos	19
34.	Steffi Graff	17
35.	Roy Jones Jr.	15
35.	Rick Mirer	15
35.	Tab Ramos	15
38.	Mike Mussina	14
39.	Arantxa Sanchez Vicario	13
40.	Darren Daulton	10
41.	Missy Giove	6
41.	Mark Phillipoussis	6
43.	Julie Foudy	4

Definition: A TRU* Score is the percentage of teens familiar with a particular celebrity who likes that celebrity "very much."

Source: Teenage Research Unlimited, Inc.

Recent popularity polls indicate that Penny stands tall among his younger fans.

TWICE AS NICE

Whether he's making people smile in his real hometown or his adopted one, Penny's living proof that it's better to give than to receive

By Ron Higgins

Y ou can tell a lot about a basketball star's character by the way he plays the game.

Michael Jordan dominates any situation. Dennis Rodman plays like he's on edge. Hakeem Olajuwon has a quiet, dignified — almost artistic — touch to his game.

Penny Hardaway? He's an unselfish giver who always does what he's asked, and then some. "Whatever you need to win, Penny gets it for you . . . he gives you heart and soul," Orlando teammate Jon Koncak says.

Hardaway's penchant for trying to make everyone around him look good — instead of taking the open shot himself — drove his high school and college coaches crazy. Orlando head coach Brian Hill felt the same way until he told Hardaway he had to look to shoot.

Penny can't help himself. He likes helping other people, and his off-the-court charity work is somehow more awe-inspiring than his no-look passes are to an arena full of Magic faithful. Few players in the NBA give as much of themselves as Hardaway does, and he does it in two cities: his actual hometown of Memphis and his adopted hometown of Orlando.

"I live and work in Orlando, and

Christmas Cheer: Penny could pass for Santa Claus if Santa was 6-7 with a killer jumper.

it's a great city," Hardaway says. "But Memphis is home, and I love coming home in the summer. I like helping my home. My mom and grandmother still live there, and it's where I'll live when I've finished my career."

When he was drafted by the Magic, Hardaway quickly established an organization in Orlando called Penny's Pals. In the past three years, the program has raised more than $100,000 each year for various charities. In Memphis, Hardaway's annual August charity game at The Pyramid raises $100,000 as well.

The 1995 game was a testament to both Hardaway's drawing power and his relationship with his fellow players. A week before the game, concerns arose that the NBA stars scheduled to attend would miss the event because of labor squabbles with the league. Although the league already had sanctioned the game, questions existed about whether players would be covered in the event of injury.

Yet when the opening ball was tossed, the gang was all there: Scottie Pippen, Nick Van Exel, Cedric Ceballos, Robert Horry, Todd Day, Elliot Perry and others. And oh yes — 20,000 fans.

On the Saturday of the game, 8,000 tickets were sold. Having worried himself sick during the week that strike talk

would hurt attendance, Hardaway was all smiles.

"Four days ago, everybody thought the players wouldn't show up," Hardaway said after the game. "But when I walked out and saw 20,000 people, it was a thrill. I had some people tell me Memphis ought to be in the NBA the way it supported this game."

Penny's Pals and his charity game are his public good deeds. But he also does some incredible things that don't draw any publicity, and he likes it that way.

Each Thanksgiving in Orlando, he buys and distributes thousands of turkeys for the underprivileged. At Christmas, he and personal assistant Greg Moore raid toy stores and buy thousands of dollars' worth of bicycles, toys and other goodies for delivery to needy children.

"When I gave away those toys and bikes, it was a better feeling than I've ever had in basketball," Hardaway says. "When I saw the faces on those kids light up, I knew I'd given them something they'd never had."

Hardaway admits he's a soft touch

Role Model: Whether playing ball or motivating kids, Penny is at his best on the court.

for helping people in need, whether it's a financial donation to send a Memphis youth AAU basketball team to a national tournament, $25,000 to construct an outdoor court in an inner-city Orlando neighborhood or simply lending money to an acquaintance who's struggling to get his life together.

"A lot of times, so many charities ask for my help that I don't know which one to help," Hardaway says. "My close friends criticize me for maybe giving someone $100 or buying them dinner. I can't help myself. When you're young, you say, 'If I ever have money, I'm going to try and help as many people as possible.' "

Moore and Penny's agents, Carl and Kevin Poston, try to help him balance his time between basketball, char-ity work, endorsements and some sem-blance of a private life.

"If I gave Penny all the requests for his time in charity work, he'd never get anything else done," Kevin Poston says. "I have to be the bad guy that tells peo-ple 'no' because Penny rarely does."

When he's home in Memphis, Penny often makes unannounced vis-its to St. Jude's Children's Research Center. The hospital special-izes in treating children with cancer. Sometimes, just seeing the patients and their distraught parents can bring a tear to even the strongest man's eye.

But Penny goes back time after time. He remembers one visit a year ago when a sick child who rarely smiled vis-ibly brightened when Hardaway entered the room. Penny sat on the child's bed and visited with him like they were old pals.

"It's amazing that such a brief visit can mean so much," Hardaway says.

Hardaway's close friends, such as Shelby County Sheriff's Deputy Randy Wade, are no strangers to his random acts of kindness.

"A couple of years ago, I got a call from this guy in Memphis who says, 'Penny told me to call you,' " Wade says. "I didn't know who this man was, but he told me. This person had just been in Orlando and his car broke down and he didn't have any money to get home to Memphis.

"The only person he knows who lives in Orlando from Memphis is Penny. This man somehow gets to Orlando Arena, finds Penny after a practice and explains his situation. Penny gives him the money to get his car fixed and tells the man to call me when he gets home to Memphis."

And the way Penny runs his annual basketball camp in Memphis is just one more example of his tireless generosity.

Penny lends more than his name to his camp. He's there every day to deliv-er an hour-long lecture about staying away from drugs and concentrating on getting an education.

He poses for individual pictures with each of the more than 300 campers — a process that takes an entire day by itself. He also autographs one item for each camper. (He's had to ask campers' parents not to get in line, too.)

Penny charges an enrollment fee for the camp, but the money pays for expenses and camp coaches, all friends or acquaintances of Penny's. Of course, Hardaway himself also pays for about

Center Court: Penny lives by a simple credo — real life first, basketball second.

A Glimpse of the Future: Some kids really want to Be Like Mike, but these Li'l Pennies have different aspirations.

100 underprivileged children to attend as well.

"We try to do it in an orderly fashion, but sometimes we'll get kids who say, 'Penny told me to come,' " camp director Jim Kern says. "I'll ask Penny and he'll say, 'Oh yeah. I told him just to come to camp.' "

During camp, Penny walks the floor. If he notices a youngster with worn basketball shoes, Hardaway gets the child's shoe size, goes to the Memphis Nike warehouse and buys a new pair for the kid.

Even before he signed with Orlando and became an NBA millionaire, Hardaway's devotion to helping others was obvious. Shortly after being drafted by the Magic, Penny was driving down Poplar Avenue in Memphis when he noticed a car had broken down in the middle lane.

As a stressed mother watched over the car and her children in the middle of the busiest street in the city, cars sped past her. But Hardaway stopped. He made sure the woman got help, then gave her money to buy her four hungry kids a nice dinner.

The woman thanked him, then stared through the darkness at him. She asked, "You're Penny Hardaway, aren't you?"

"Yes ma'am," Penny answered. Then he drove off in the darkness, happy once again to provide an assist. •

Ron Higgins is a sportswriter for The Commercial Appeal *in Memphis, Tenn.*

Portraits
of
Penny

Anfernee Hardaway's

on-court versatility

provides a variety of

references for artists

intent on capturing

his persona on canvas

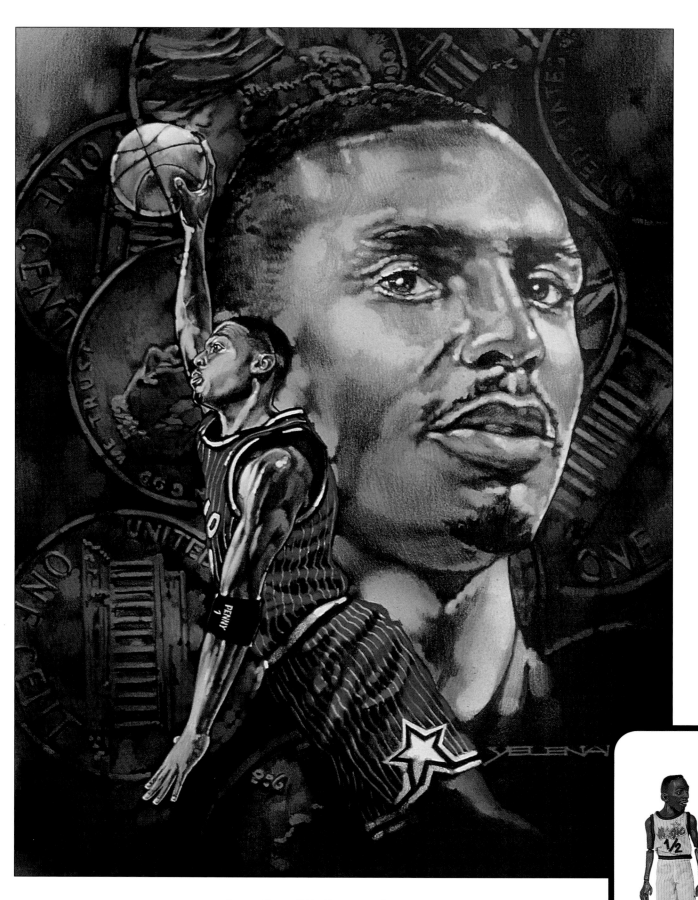

Andy Yelenak **Watercolor**

George Humes **Mixed Media**

Reginald Gay oil

A PENNY

Penny Hardaway's upbringing —
and a random act of violence —
taught him two lessons:
Always be careful, and
always listen to your
grandmother

By Ron Higgins

Strong family support
from his grandmother,
Louise, and mother,
Fae, put Penny on the
right path.

April 28, 1991, will stay with Anfernee Hardaway forever. That night, the Memphis State freshman learned to appreciate having grown up in the care of his strict, caring and always protective grandmother.

At 9:35 p.m., Hardaway and a friend had just pulled into the driveway of Hardaway's cousin, LaMarcus Golden. A car that had been circling the block stopped. A man asked directions and then pulled a gun. He ordered Hardaway and his friend onto the ground, then robbed them of money, sneakers and jewelry.

"I kept thinking, 'He's going to shoot me in the back. He's going to shoot me in the back of the head,' " Hardaway says. "We stood up when they drove off, and they started shooting. I was trying to jump in the hatchback and I just got one foot up when I got hit. The bullet ricocheted off the pavement where I thought about diving. If I would have [dived], I would have been hit in the head."

As it was, the budding basketball star escaped with a bullet wound and three broken bones in his right foot — a reminder, even at age 18, of how fortunate he was in his younger years to have been raised under Louise Hardaway's watchful eyes.

BEFORE Penny entered the
first grade, his mother, Fae, left for California to pursue a singing career. Though she visited every Christmas, Fae didn't return full-time until Penny was in the eighth grade. His father wasn't around.

"I named him Anfernee because I wanted him to have a name like no one else," Fae says. "I wanted his name to be odd so that people would always remember it. I made sure Anfernee let other kids know his name wasn't Anthony."

The raising of Anfernee was left to grandmother Louise, who called her grandson "Pretty." The Southern drawl pronunciation of "Puitty" sounded like "Penny." The nickname stuck.

In a shotgun shack at 2977 Forrest St. in Memphis, where as many as nine people lived at once with uncles, aunts and cousins stopping by, Louise and Penny survived. He shared a bed with his grandmother until he got his own fold-out bed in her room when he was 9.

Penny remembers his grandmother as a strong disciplinarian whose priority was his safety. She made sure he was at Early Grove Baptist Church every Sunday and at home every night by his curfew.

"I used to stand at my door and watch other kids in the neighborhood run the streets while I'd have to be home at 10," Penny recalls. "I'd cry because I'd hated it so much. She said, 'You'll thank me for this when you grow.' She was right.

"I probably could have started smoking or drinking like a lot of those kids. Every time I see someone with drugs, I say, 'That could have been me.' Every time I see my grandmother, I thank her."

Grandma's rules were simple: no cussing, get top grades in school, homework before TV, don't be messy and wake up early, even on non-school days.

She always kept an eye out for him. When he went to Treadwell High, she was the head cook at the school's cafeteria. She even rode the school bus with him.

"I had a key to our house made, put it on a chain, and he

In 1991, a bullet stole Penny's innocence and broke three bones in his foot.

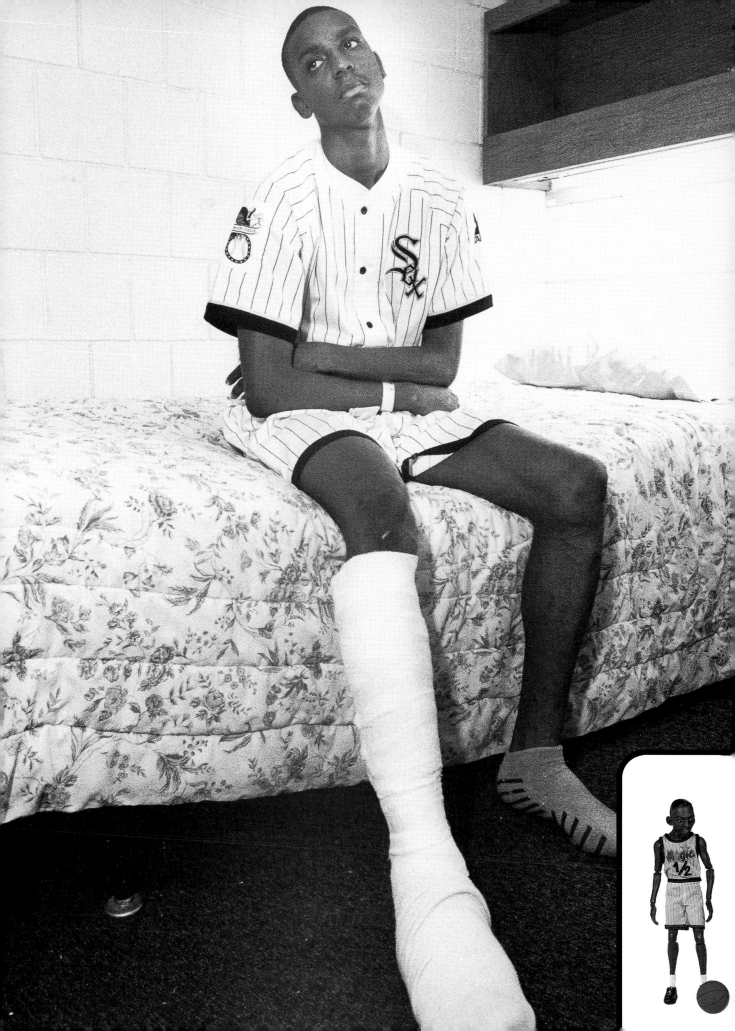

wore it around his neck," Louise says. "I wanted him to be able to get in the house if he beat me home."

But soon, Penny had an after-school diversion: basketball. His gravitation toward hoops just sort of happened, even though his first love was football. Penny loved the Dallas Cowboys and had their whole uniform, from helmet to cleats.

But Louise steered him away from football when she and Penny watched it on TV one day, and he explained the game. Ever the guardian of Penny's well-being, Louise told him there was no way he would play football.

"We had a basketball goal in our backyard, but you couldn't drag me out of the house to play basketball," Hardaway says. "I don't know what really changed me over to basketball."

PENNY started showing up at com-

munity centers where some of Memphis' finest basketball players honed their skills. His game, physical talent and natural feel stuck out immediately. So did his work ethic and quiet demeanor.

"Even when the gym wasn't open on Sundays, Penny would come around and play on the outside court," says Paul Henderson, who worked at Lester Community Center, where Penny played. "He was quiet, but everyone liked Penny."

As a ninth grader at Treadwell High, Penny's role model was senior Elliot Perry, who went on to star at Memphis State before Hardaway and now plays for the Milwaukee Bucks.

Perry was serious about his game and his grades. He couldn't excel in one without the other.

"I watched how Elliot handled recruiting and how serious he was about his schoolwork," Hardaway says. "He had school

WONDER YEARS

Penny's stats at Memphis Treadwell High School:

Season	G	PTS	AVG
1986-87	25	271	10.8
1987-88	30	717	23.9
1988-89	40	1,289	32.2
1989-90	21	762	36.3

Penny's high school accomplishments:

- **Parade Magazine National High School Player of the Year (1990)**

- **First-team All-America selection by Basketball Times (1990)**

- **Preseason All-America selection by Dick Vitale, Street & Smith's, Blue Ribbon Magazine (1989)**

- **Memphis Player of the Year (twice)**

- **All-Metro pick (three times)**

- **All-Region, All-District (four times)**

Penny proved he had the makings of a star during his prep days at Memphis Treadwell.

books with him all the time."

But despite Perry's example and even with his friend and AAU coach Jim Kern pushing him about his grades, Hardaway was declared ineligible for six weeks during his senior season. He didn't lack intelligence; he just got lazy.

His grades kept him from playing for the first time in his high school career. Coincidentally, another player's grade troubles helped Penny earn his starting spot three years earlier.

"Anfernee wanted to play junior high ball [in the ninth grade], but I lost a varsity player at the end of the second six weeks because of ineligibility," Treadwell head coach Garnie Currie Jr. says. "I asked all of my players, 'Who wants to start?' Anfernee raised his hand.

"Being skinny made him awkward, but he had the ability to create when a play broke down. Everything he does now — dribbling between the legs, no-look passes — he did here. I wanted people to see his game. I never tried to contain him."

Not that he could have if he had tried. Heck, no one could contain Penny in high school. By the time he graduated, Penny was second in Shelby County history with 36.3 points per game and fourth with 622 career assists and 3,039 points. He holds the county record for points in a game with 58 against Mitchell in the 1989-90 season.

"He was always very focused," Currie says. "Our relationship was good and bad. I tried to be a coach and father figure, and he might have resented it. We pushed him and pushed him."

Perry also admired Hardaway's development: "Penny never had a mother and a father at every game like a lot of us did. He leaned on his grandmother and she did a lot for him."

PENNY hasn't forgotten how much his grandmother did. After becoming a pro, Penny bought Louise a spacious house on four acres in East Memphis. Whether it's the NBA Finals, All-Star Games or the Olympics, it's a good bet his grandmother and/or his mother have been flown in to watch him play.

One of the first commercial endorsements Hardaway did was for King Cotton, a Memphis-based meat-packing plant that made the hot dogs and lunch meats his grandmother served him as a child. The reason for the endorsement? Penny was able to get his grandmother in the commercial.

Penny disappointed himself and his grandmother when his grades sidelined him again — this time when he was a freshman at Memphis State — but he made up for it by working so hard he was on the Dean's List before he left school after his junior year.

Hardaway has never forgotten his roots. One of the first things he did as a pro was to become spokesman for the Shelby County Sheriff's Department in its drug-awareness efforts. A survey showed Hardaway's presence was strong; 90 percent of Memphis and Shelby County school children were aware of the campaign.

"It keeps me grounded to what's important in life," Penny says. "You can only buy so many things for yourself and people around you. It's all about giving yourself back. I love that."

And by giving back to Memphis, he just might make the streets a little safer for the next generation of basketball superstars. After all, not everyone has a grandmother like Louise Hardaway.   •

Ron Higgins is a sportswriter for The Commercial Appeal *in Memphis, Tenn.*

By the time he made the starting lineup at Memphis State, Penny's talents came through loud and clear.

KAZA

The Magic carpet ride for Penny and his Orlando teammates hit a snag when Shaq suddenly changed

AM!

addresses. Now, the best one-two punch in the league is a continent apart. **By Ron Higgins**

ANDREW D. BERNSTEIN / NBA PHOTOS

enny Hardaway's basketball relationship with Shaquille O'Neal ended the same way it started: with a gold medal. And although victories marked their first and last moments as teammates, Penny and Shaq didn't enjoy nearly as much success as the Orlando Magic — and their fans — had expected.

United for the first time on the gold medal-winning South squad at the 1990 Olympic Festival, Penny and Shaq truly were a dynamic duo. Their partnership grew on the set of a motion picture and blossomed in Orlando when Penny joined Shaq in the big fella's second season in the NBA.

With three Atlantic Division titles and an NBA Finals berth in just three seasons, they appeared destined to become the Magic and Kareem of the '90s.

That destiny unraveled when the Lakers lured O'Neal away from Orlando with a seven-year, $120 million deal. The 1996 Olympics became a farewell tour of sorts for the young

Penny and Shaq ended their tenure as teammates with an Olympic gold medal, but they never

tandem. Penny thought the Games would be the happiest time of his life; the camaraderie of a Dream Team, a gold-medal triumph in front of the home crowd, a chance to shine on the global stage.

But when Hardaway heard the news of Shaq's decision at 7 a.m. July 18 — Penny's 24th birthday — he was crestfallen.

"I was devastated. I hardly talked to anybody," Penny says. "My gut feeling was that he was going to stay. I was in shock. I guess what Shaq had to do was business. He feels comfortable out in Los Angeles. I knew he loved the city.

It was his dream to play there and he fulfilled it."

Rumors of a rift between Hardaway and O'Neal weren't uncommon, but Penny brushes them aside the way he would a rookie defender. Before Hardaway returned to Memphis after the Bulls swept the Magic in the '96 playoffs, he stopped at O'Neal's house for dinner.

"We're not the best of friends; we don't hang out with each other," Hardaway says. "But we have respect for each other's game. If there's jealousy between us, it's news to me."

O'Neal did not bother immediately telling Hardaway he had signed with the Lakers. But

managed to win an NBA title. Now, Penny will go for it solo.

NATHANIEL S. BUTLER / NBA PHOTOS

when Shaq finally did, Penny said he spent about "two minutes with me, wishing me good luck and hoping I got a contract I wanted in the future."

"I told Penny he was going to be a great player, and he seemed to understand my decision," O'Neal says.

The Hardaway-O'Neal combination might never have debuted in the NBA had it not been for Shaq's pull with Magic management. By the time Shaq started tearing down backboards for the Magic, he was well aware of Penny's talents.

When they played together in the '90 Olympic Festival, Hardaway led all players in assists and steals. "I remember he was a great passer," Shaq says. "When I was open, the ball was there."

They rekindled their partnership after Hardaway's junior (and final) season at Memphis, when they played basketball prospects recruited by a high-profile college coach (Nick Nolte) in *Blue Chips*.

During pickup games between takes, O'Neal realized Hardaway was an ideal fit for the Magic. He phoned Orlando player personnel director

With Shaq at his side, Penny rarely called attention to himself. Now that Shaquille is Hollywood-boun

John Gabriel and told him Hardaway could be the solution to the team's playoff puzzle.

Hardaway's initial workout with Orlando wasn't impressive, but he and his agents, Carl and Kevin Poston, persuaded the team to let Hardaway practice again two days before the NBA draft.

That workout with several Magic veterans is the stuff of Orlando lore, and the Magic decided to trade No. 1 pick Chris Webber to Golden State for No. 3 choice Hardaway and a trio of first-round picks.

"We were staggered," Orlando general man-ager Pat Williams says. "I saw a dozen things that would have had a full house ripping seats from the building. I'd never seen a team throw out all their thinking 24 hours before a draft. It was so bizarre."

Hardaway — not O'Neal — became the Magic's first All-NBA first-team player. And Hardaway — not O'Neal — became the Magic fans' choice as most popular player.

While Shaq seemed larger than life, mug-ging for Pepsi and Reebok, Hardaway quietly worked on his game and limited his endorse-ments until his Nike campaign this past season

wever, Penny's going to have to speak up.

GOING SOLO

In his three years in the NBA, Penny's played just 32 regular season games without O'Neal. Here's how he fared:

G	AST	AVG	REB	AVG	PTS	AVG
Without Shaquille						
32	205	6.4	157	4.9	827	25.8
With Shaquille						
209	1,472	7.0	972	4.7	3,879	18.6
Totals						
241	1,677	7.0	1,129	4.7	4,706	19.5

NATHANIEL S. BUTLER / NBA PHOTOS

with alter-ego puppet Li'l Penny proved immensely popular.

Being named an Olympian certified Penny's superstardom, a level of hype Shaq had reached years ago. Hardaway enjoyed his Olympic experience as the consummate team player.

"Just to go to the gym and see people chanting 'U-S-A' makes you feel great," Hardaway says. "It may be the biggest honor I've ever had. Just the opening ceremonies were worth it."

Away from the Olympic court, however, Hardaway felt like a prisoner. The suffocating crowds would have been enough, but security was tighter than normal. Then a pipe bomb exploded in Centennial Park next to the team hotel. A few days later, the hotel itself had a bomb threat, leading to an evacuation.

The events completed a trifecta of Olympic bombshells that started with O'Neal's decision to sign with the Lakers. But when he was on the court, Hardaway tried to concentrate on winning gold and not on his Shaq-less future.

"If I didn't focus on what I was doing, I would have cheated myself and I would have cheated my country," Penny says. "I knew when the Games were over I'd start working out

Orlando's Dynamic Duo catapulted the Magic from the Eastern Conference cellar to the NBA Finals

THE WAY THEY WERE

Some random facts about the now-defunct Penny-Shaq tandem:

- In the 1994-95 season, Penny and Shaq combined to average 50.2 points per game, the most for a duo in the league. The duo finished second to Michael Jordan and Scottie Pippen in 1995-96.

- Penny earned NBA Player of the Month honors for November 1995, leading the team to a 13-2 record while Shaq was out with an injury.

- In their three seasons as teammates, Penny and Shaq were voted to start the All-Star Game together twice.

- In the last three seasons, Orlando is 2-3 in games Penny missed and 22-10 in games Shaq missed.

- One or both of the duo led the Magic in scoring in 60 of the team's 82 games in 1995-96.

- Penny and Shaq accounted for 272 of the team's 387 dunks in 1995-96.

extremely hard and figure out what to do from there."

Hardaway says Gabriel called him later in the day on his birthday and promised the Magic would recover from Shaq's departure.

"Gabe told me, 'The big fella is gone now. This is your team,'" Penny says. "He said, 'We're going to try and get you some help in the middle. . . . We wish Shaq the best and we have to try and move on.' He didn't bash Shaq."

Several days after Penny's birthday, he final-

ly felt happy enough to have a party. The Olympics turned out to be a long two weeks for Penny, knowing the championship game would be his last as a teammate of O'Neal's. He also had to endure the verbal jabs of Olympic teammates who told him that without Shaq, the Magic would probably lose enough to fall into the lottery.

When the Olympic flame was extinguished, Hardaway had won a gold medal, but he'd lost his top teammate. Sometimes, the victor doesn't get all of the spoils.   •

Ron Higgins is a sportswriter for The Commercial Appeal *in Memphis, Tenn.*

before Shaq could say "Kazaam!"

Penny Hardaway's

contributions

and enthusiasm

for the NBA

All-Star Weekend

make him . . .

. . . aStaram

By Bill Fay

ongStars

s a three-time All-Star, Anfernee Hardaway prefers anonymity.

As he takes his place among the stars of the NBA, he defers to his peers. He almost apologizes for being called the best at his position.

Take, for example, his thoughts after the inaugural Rookie All-Star Game, played in Minneapolis in 1994.

He was named Most Valuable Player after scoring 22 points. He dunked. He glided effortlessly through the lane for layups. He even knocked down a couple of three-pointers just for good measure.

Yet his team lost, 74-68. The star for the winners was then-Golden State forward Chris Webber, the only double double performer in the game (18 points and 10 rebounds). The fact that Webber and Hardaway had been linked tightly ever since they were traded for each other on draft night in 1993 made the story all the more compelling.

"People are always going to try and compare us, but we were just out there to have fun," Hardaway insists. "It wasn't me and Chris trying to beat each other, but I'm sure the media and fans were asking themselves before the game who was going to do better."

Members of the media had their say, giving Hardaway the MVP Award in a near unanimous vote. Webber was very good that night, but Hardaway was great and the award justified. Still, the Magic's man felt compelled to downplay the whole deal.

"There was enough defense being played to stop people if they wanted, but it's not like guys were playing playoff defense or anything," Hardaway said after hitting eight of nine shots in the game.

"And really, I'd rather be distributing the ball than shooting it all the time."

That's exactly what he did at the 1995 All-Star Game in Phoenix, handing out a team-high 11 assists. Hardaway played more minutes (31) than anyone on the East team and spent most of the afternoon trying to make his teammates look good.

Hardaway provided some special service to his Orlando teammate, Shaquille O'Neal. O'Neal had been humbled a year earlier at the All-Star Game in Minneapolis when the West ganged up on him, forcing the big guy into a 2 of 12 shooting day. But in this game, Hardaway created easy opportunities for Shaq, who responded with a more characteristic 9 of 16 shooting performance.

While feeding his monsterous center felt good, being voted to the starting lineup by the fans was Penny's most cherished memory. In fact, he was the top vote-getter among the guards, leading the balloting from start to finish at his position.

"I know some people like to knock the fans vote, but as a player, it really does a lot for your confidence to know the whole country thinks you're one of the best in the league," Hardaway says. "I was just hoping that maybe the coaches would vote me onto the team, but when I realized I was going to make it because of the fans, that turned it into a real thrill."

Get used to it, Penny

It's like a two-way street. As a top star, Penny thrills fans nationwide. In return, the fans reward Penny by stuffing the ballot box with votes for him to appear at the next All-Star Game.

The fans voted him in again for the 1996 All-Star Game in San Antonio. But this time, the thrill was who he was voted to play alongside: Michael Jordan, one of his idols while growing up on the

Although Hardaway's Sensations lost to the Phenoms in the first-ever NBA Rookie All-Star Game, Penny won MVP honors with a 22-point performance.

Even at All-Star games, Hardaway, at just 6-7, is not afraid to attack the basket against the best big men in the league

shiningBrightamongthestars

Penny Hardaway has dazzled fans and peers alike with his outstanding play during All-Star weekends. The following is a statistical look at his performances in his three All-Star appearances:

Season	Min.	FGM	FGA	Pct.	FTM	FTA	Pct.	Reb.	Ast.	Pts.
1994-*#	22	8	9	.889	4	6	.667	1	3	22
1995	31	4	9	.444	4	6	.667	5	11	12
1996	31	6	8	.750	4	4	1.000	3	7	18
Totals	84	18	26	.692	12	16	.750	9	21	52
Averages	28							3	7	17.3

* - Schick Rookie Game
\# - Named game's MVP

playgrounds of Memphis.

Hardaway had spoken often during his rookie season of his disappointment that the Bulls' superstar had retired just before the start of that season. When Jordan returned to the NBA 18 months later, Hardaway was in awe. Now, he was to join him in the backcourt for an All-Star Game.

Just to make sure Hardaway didn't forget the experience, Jordan pulled a memorable practical joke on his protege. As the players were being introduced at San Antonio's Alamodome, Jordan secretly unsnapped most of Hardaway's warmup pants, then stuck his foot on the pants leg so that when Hardaway trotted out in front of the national TV cameras, his pants came tumbling down for all the nation to see.

"He got me that time, got me bad," Hardaway says. "But it was still an honor to play with Michael Jordan. He's probably the greatest player to ever play the game and there I was in All-Star Game right alongside him.

"It's a day I'll never forget."

It's a day many fans won't forget either, as they watched Hardaway scorch the West defense for 18 points and seven assists, several of which were directed to

the Bulls' star.

Hardaway took one other thing home from that experience, again courtesy of Jordan. He spent some time with MJ and came away with the realization that part of the reason Jordan is the best is because he thinks he's the best. He won't take a backseat to anyone.

"I love the All-Star Game because you meet the guys who are at the top of your profession and you learn so much more about the game from them," Hardaway says. "I got a lot from my first All-Star experience from Joe Dumars and Michael was just great last year. After talking to him, I feel like even though it's an honor to play against him, he thinks it's a big deal to play against me, too. He thinks that's a challenge."

It has become a challenge faced not only by Jordan, but by the rest of the league as well. And it is a challenge that Penny should present every February he's in the league.

Bill Fay covers the Magic for The Tampa Tribune.

Magic II

When Magic Johnson went one-on-one against Penny Hardaway for the first time, he thought he was looking into a mirror

By Tim Povtak

Magic Johnson was a symbol of international success and a member of the legendary 1992 Dream Team when he took his first extensive look at Penny Hardaway.

The wiry 19-year-old guard from Memphis State was part of the U.S. Developmental Team, which was offered as fodder to help the Dream Team prepare for the Olympics.

Johnson, 33, already had won his five NBA titles with the Lakers, virtually revolutionized the game, retired once, then returned to lead the greatest basketball team ever assembled.

But a crazy thing happened the first time the two teams scrimmaged . . . the Developmental Team won and the pupil outplayed the master.

"When I played against Penny, I thought I was looking in the mirror and playing against myself. It was amazing," Johnson recalls. "He [Hardaway] impressed me. And I don't impress very easily."

Of course, the next time they scrimmaged, the Dream Team rolled, and Johnson spanked Hardaway like a naughty child. But it was an experience neither player ever forgot. The King and His Heir — Magic and Penny — would forever be linked.

Since the Magic Man burst into the league in 1979 as a 6-9, 205-pound point guard, NBA scouts have been searching high and low for another like him. Hardaway finally might be the one.

Like Magic, Penny is a tall (6-7), unselfish point guard with tremendous instincts, court vision and savvy. Like Magic, Penny is so versatile he can plug himself into any situation and respond with an All-Star performance.

"I can see where people compare Penny to Magic Johnson," says Hardaway's teammate, Dennis Scott. "He does whatever he feels the team needs to be successful. Because he's so versatile, he can do almost anything."

Like Magic, Penny can score at will. In fact, Hardaway might be a more advanced offensive force at this stage of his career than his predecessor. It took time for Magic to develop his perimeter game. Of course, once he did, he became unstoppable. Penny's outside gunning was top rate from the moment he stepped on the court.

No one ever will distribute the ball better than Magic. But Penny sure comes close. No point guard can rebound like Magic. But Penny definitely can clean the glass. Like Magic, Penny plays with a special flair that electrifies an arena. And both are known more by their nicknames than their actual first names.

Most importantly, Magic and Penny share the same motto: winning is everything.

"Every so often, a player comes into the league with a 'special' label on him," says Magic head coach Brian Hill. "That doesn't happen very often. But I think Penny had that from Day One. It was something you could see from the start."

Although their styles are similar, one distinct difference exists. Magic's trademark smile lit up basketball arenas from coast to coast. Hardaway rarely cracks a smile, displaying a seriousness that belies his youthful eagerness.

Still, No. 32 loves what he sees when he watches No. 1 hit the court.

"He knows how to use his teammates very well," Johnson explains. "He knows how to be in control without really

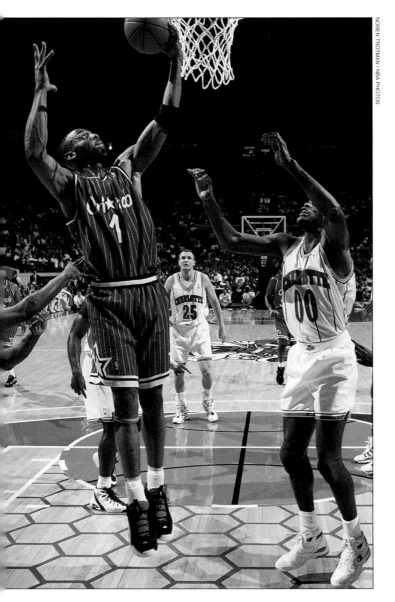

NOREN TROTMAN / NBA PHOTOS

Comparisons between Penny and Magic extend beyond offense. Like Magic, Penny rebounds well and plays solid defense against top NBA guards.

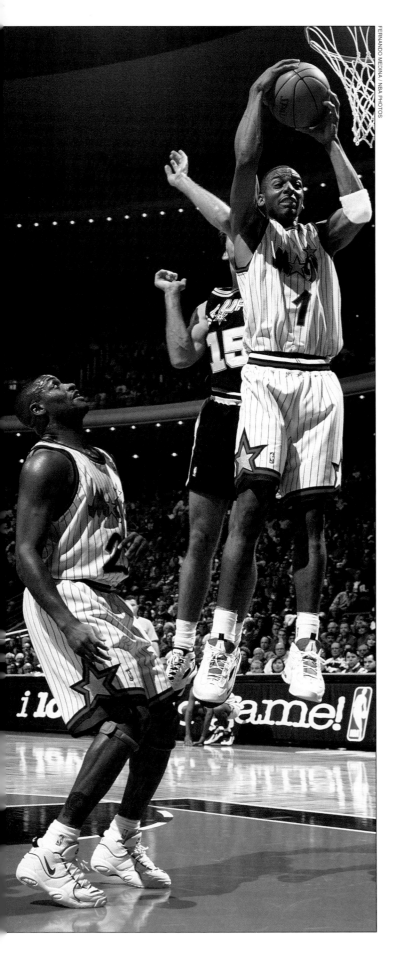

controlling people. I like that. I like the way he plays."

Hardaway's game could change significantly because of the departure of center Shaquille O'Neal — coincidentally to Magic's old turf in L.A.

With Penny and Shaq playing together for three seasons, the comparisons to Magic and Kareem Abdul-Jabbar were constant. Now, without his big man, Penny must carry more of the load.

"To this point, he always tailored his game to fit in with his center," Johnson says. "And he did that well. That's how I did it in the early years with Kareem. You hold your game back for the betterment of the team because you've got a big, dominant center. That's the sign of a great player. Now, he has to let it all out."

Johnson says Hardaway shouldn't have a problem with increased scoring duties. Actually, he says, Penny might be more suited to playing shooting guard than point.

"I think now he could be the next Michael more than the next Magic," Johnson says. "He can do more than I ever could. I think he could become the next prolific scorer in this league."

The numbers seem to back up Magic's prediction. Hardaway's scoring average has climbed in each of his three seasons. He averaged 16 points as a rookie, 20.9 points in his second season and 21.7 in his third when O'Neal missed 28 games and the Magic won 60. Hardaway expects to average considerably more without O'Neal in the lineup.

By comparison, Johnson averaged 18 points as a rookie and 21.6 points in his second season. His scoring average dipped in the next several years, then leaped back to a career high of 23.9 points in his eighth season when Abdul-Jabbar's game began to decline.

"I think Penny could be one of those scorers who you just can't stop, like Michael in a scaled down way," Johnson says. "I just think he's better suited now to be a two-guard because he likes the ball brought to him. He's still making plays, but he makes them from the scoring position."

Hardaway is flattered and somewhat embarrassed by the comparisons to his idols Magic and Michael. Obviously, he knows he has a long way to go.

"I think the comparisons started immediately because I was a tall guard like Magic," Hardaway says. "I've always admired his game, but I don't think I tried to pattern mine after his. We're not the same. I haven't won yet, either, so I'm not anywhere in that class. Maybe someday."

Magic and Michael have voiced their praises of Penny's game. Comparisons aside, Penny knows he must win an NBA title to reach their level.

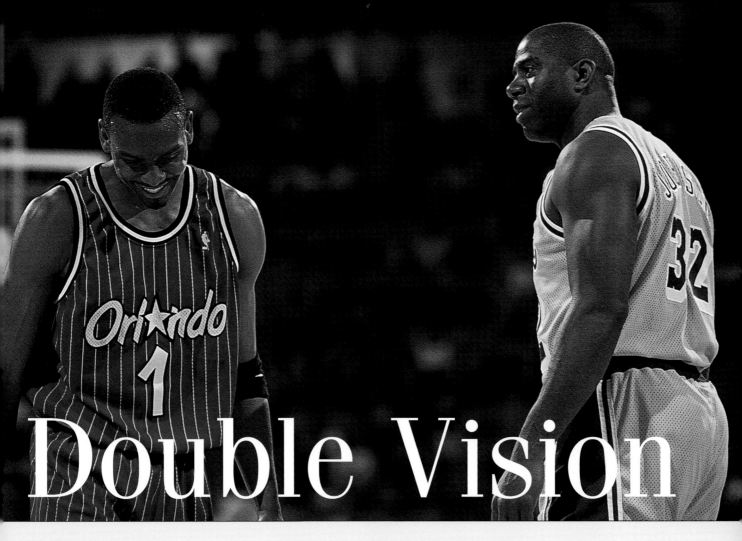

Double Vision

Magic Johnson and Penny Hardaway may not look alike, but their statistics through their first three NBA seasons sure do

Player	Age	Games	Assists	Avg.	Points	Avg.
Penny Hardaway	24	241	1,677	7.0	4,706	19.5
Magic Johnson	22	192	1,623	8.5	3,632	18.9

Although Johnson started his career as a point guard, his versatility allowed him to play almost any position on the floor. In his rookie season, he even moved to center for an injured Abdul-Jabbar in the playoffs. Johnson also switched to forward when the Lakers needed him. And when he returned briefly in the 1995-96 season after a four-year retirement, he came back as a point power forward hybrid.

Hardaway possesses that same kind of versatility. In fact, even before O'Neal left for Los Angeles, Hardaway speculated on playing at small forward and at shooting guard, depending upon which Orlando teammate is playing well.

"Sometimes, the best team we can put on the floor may be with me at different positions," Hardaway admits. "That's something I've been wanting to do. The top players can do that. And now, maybe it's time."

Magic believes the time IS now.

"Penny is just starting to blossom," Johnson says. "And I want to be around to see what happens. When they take the cap off his bottle, that's going to be some fine tasting cola." •

Tim Povtak covers the Magic for The Orlando Sentinel.

Proving
HIS
Point

As today's young point guards take on a new and more dynamic role in the NBA, Anfernee Hardaway stands out as the state-of-the-art blueprint

By Tim Povtak

There once was a time when point guards were almost an afterthought in the NBA, when the game was ruled by the big men and the playmakers were considered interchangeable.

That was before this '90s crop of backcourt stars — led by Anfernee Hardaway — changed the position and changed the game. They've given up the backseat for their role in leading the league into the next century.

Hardaway, Gary Payton, Jason Kidd and Damon

Michael will tell you that Penny's a do-it-all point guard.

Stoudamire have proven the value of the new-style point guard. Centers don't dominate the game anymore. Point guards do.

No longer content with feeding the big men, today's point guards are marked by their versatility. They can score, assist, rebound and defend. They control the ball and the game.

Of all the bright young point guards in the league today, no one does it all better

than Hardaway, the classic example of the '90s point guard, the model for others to follow.

"Penny Hardaway could be the most exciting player in basketball," says Pat Williams, Orlando's vice-president. "He's just special. Every time he touches the ball, you can't take your eyes off him because you know something exciting could happen."

Hardaway, 24, already has captured the acclaim as the game's best point guard. He was named first-team All-NBA each of the last two seasons. His scoring average has climbed in each of his three seasons in the league, from 16 to 20.9 to 21.7 points. His assists average has fluctuated from 6.6 to 7.2 to 7.1. And his rebounding has leveled off, from 5.4 his first season, to 4.4 and 4.3 the next two.

His athleticism, versatility, court awareness and mental approach to the game allow him to sparkle on the

Penny excels in taking the ball in amongst the trees . . .

court. Payton, Kidd, Stoudamire and others such as Kenny Anderson, Terrell Brandon and Mookie Blaylock all possess some of his qualities, but none package it all so well. Hardaway is

. . . and in a post-up game against smaller defenders.

6-7, 215 pounds and jumps exceptionally well. He also plays with a confidence that other young point guards often lack.

"Penny is just so outstanding, and that's why I like playing against him," Payton said when the two played together on the U.S. Olympic team. "I love watching his game, learning from it. You always enjoy playing against a great talent like him. It brings out the best in everybody else. He can do it all. And at times, there is just no stopping him."

Payton, entering his seventh season, boosted the Sonics into the NBA Finals with his fine play last season. He averaged 19.3 points and 7.5 assists. He led the league with 2.85 steals. His quick hands can make opponents miserable if they aren't at the top of their game. But at 6-4, Payton doesn't quite have Hardaway's size or athleticism. He doesn't shoot or distribute the ball as well, yet he may be considered the second-best point guard in the NBA this season.

Kidd, a third-year pro, possesses the same kind of versatility and court awareness of Hardaway. His shot, quickness and size, though, just don't match up against Hardaway. Kidd recorded nine triple doubles last season, which by far was the most of any point guard. And

one of his biggest admirers is Hardaway.

"He's amazing with all those triple doubles," Hardaway says. "The way he rebounds for his size is incredible. He's so active on the offensive boards, and that's one reason he's so good at the guard spot. He also really understands the game."

Kidd averaged 16.6 points, 7.7 assists and 5.4 rebounds last season. The Mavericks finished a woeful 25-56 last season, but they were 19-9 in games that Kidd scored at least 20 points.

Stoudamire, averaged 19 points, 9.3 assists and four rebounds — Good enough to claim Rookie of the Year Honors and provide the Toronto Raptors with memorable first season. Stoudamire went through the usual rookie growing pains, but he proved a real pain to those trying to contain him.

Stoudamire, just 5-10, 171 pounds, displays great quickness. His size limits his defensive options, making him vulnerable to bigger point guards such as Hardaway. Stoudamire also

must learn to balance his own scoring against the value of keeping his teammates involved.

Others such as Anderson, Brandon and Blaylock, all are a step below, but they still came into the league with reputations as point guards who could do more

FERNANDO MEDINA

Philadelphia 76ers made Georgetown's Allen Iverson the No. 1 overall pick, recognizing the importance of the great point guard. He was the first point guard picked No. 1 since Magic Johnson in 1979. Georgia Tech point guard Stephon Marbury was taken fourth by Milwaukee, then traded to Minnesota.

In the late '80s and early '90s, the league's best point guards were players such as John Stockton, Mark Price and Tim Hardaway, smaller point guards who came into the league without much fanfare.

Because of the likes of Hardaway, point guards have taken the spotlight now, dominating action from the perimeter. Outside of Magic Johnson, there hasn't been a point guard since Oscar Robertson in 1964 to win the league's Most Valuable Player Award.

Yet Hardaway moves into this 1996-97 season as one of the early favorites to challenge Michael Jordan for league MVP honors. When Hardaway lost center Shaquille O'Neal to the Los Angeles Lakers, he realized he must do more than ever to keep the Magic in contention. And he appears ready for that challenge.

He wants the ball in his hands — at the end of the game and throughout the game. He appears eager to

than just pass the ball to the right person.

"There are some really great point guards who have come into the league lately," says Marty Blake, NBA director of scouting. "And the great ones, I've said many times, are born. They aren't made. Those are the best ones."

Recent NBA drafts reflect the increased emphasis on point guards. The '80s were filled with teams drafting front-court players quickly even though they weren't as good or as athletic as the point guards. But that thinking has changed.

In the entire decade of the '80s, just two true point guards (Isiah Thomas, 1981 and Kenny Smith, 1987) were chosen among the top seven picks in the NBA drafts. By contrast in the '90s, seven point guards already have been taken among those top

seven picks.

Seattle drafted Payton second overall in 1990. New Jersey took Anderson with the second overall pick one year later. Golden State drafted Hardaway with the No. 3 pick in '93, then immediately traded him to Orlando. Dallas chose Kidd with the second overall pick in '94, and Stoudamire (Toronto) was seventh in '95.

In the 1996 draft, the

. . . while Penny still learns from assist master, John Stockton.

accept the role as leader, the guy who must carry the Magic in the battle for Eastern Conference supremacy.

Penny didn't come into the league as a pure point guard. At Memphis State, he played almost every position while trying to help his team win games. Even in his rookie season, he played more at shooting guard while he learned the NBA. In just a few short seasons, he's become the best at what he does.

He no longer wants to be known as the best young point guard in the league. He wants to be the league's best player.

"You know how they say about Michael Jordan, that he's the best to ever play the game," Hardaway says. "Well, someday, I want them to say that about me."

Hardaway may never reach the plateau on which Jordan has peaked, but his continued excellence will solidify his place among the greatest point guards the game has seen.   •

T i m Povtak covers the Magic for The Orlando Sentinel.

ONE ON ONE

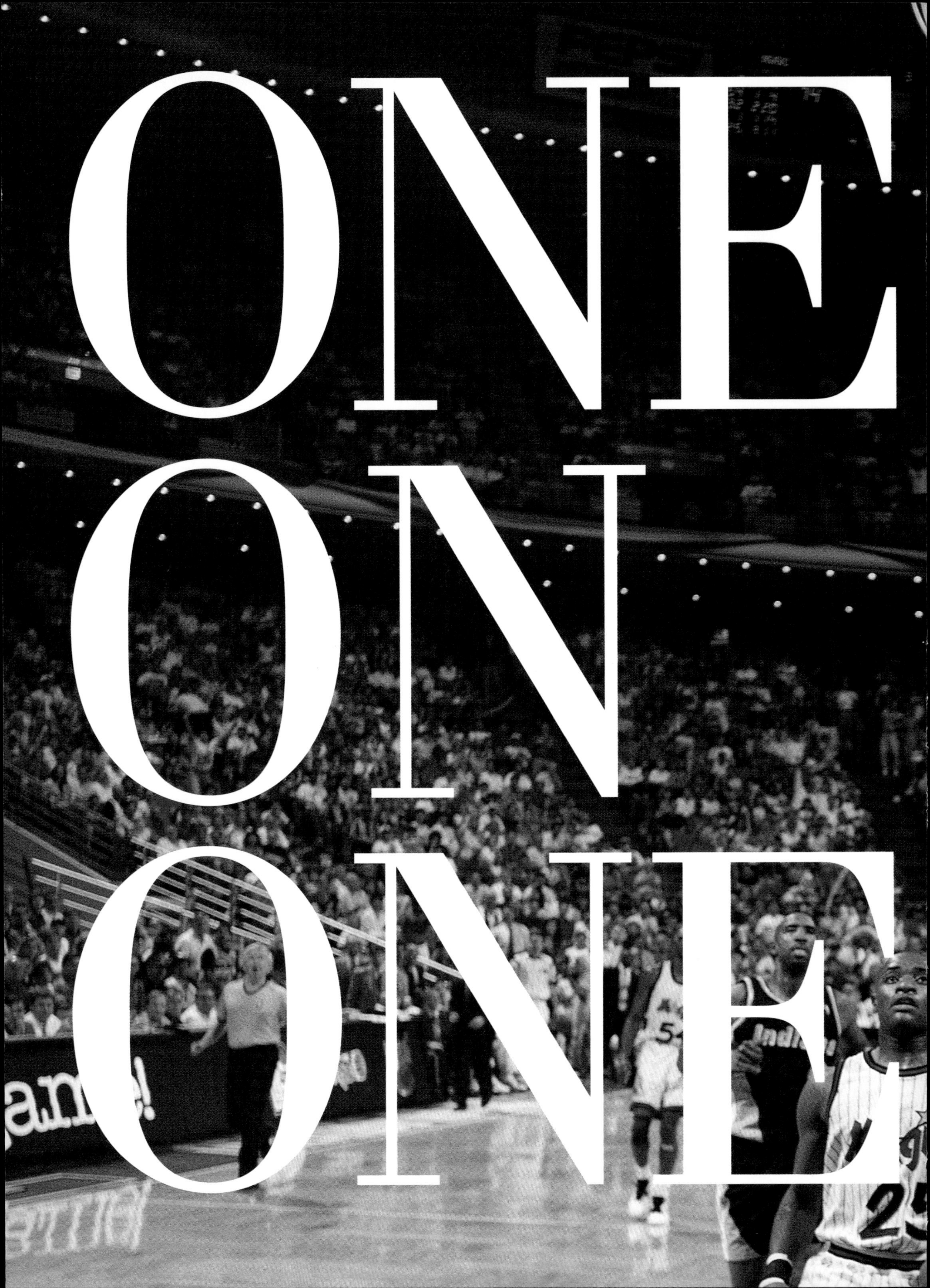

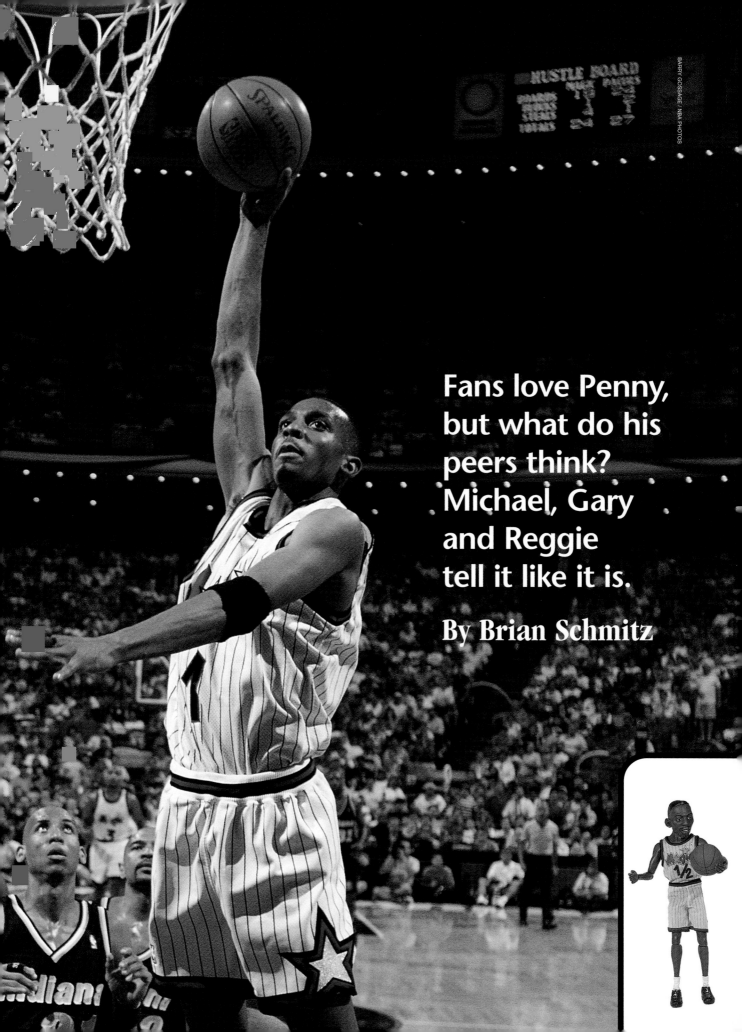

Fans love Penny,
but what do his
peers think?
Michael, Gary
and Reggie
tell it like it is.

By Brian Schmitz

MICHAEL JORDAN

Nov. 14, 1995, is a day that cleared up any confusion over who will fill Michael Jordan's role as the game's best player once he abdicates the throne.

In a head-to-head matchup against His Airness, Penny Hardaway showed why he soon will be fitted for the crown.

It was just the second week of the season when the Chicago Bulls came to the Orlando Arena to face the Magic, who were playing without superstar center Shaquille O'Neal. O'Neal had been sidelined by a broken thumb, leaving Hardaway to lead his team into battle against the league's strongest team and the league's best player.

The pregame hype of this nationally televised contest centered on the matchup between the teams' two All-Star guards.

In the locker room prior to the game, Jordan displayed his usual cool and confident self. But deep inside, the Bulls' guard had to have felt a twitch of concern about Hardaway's explosive capabilities.

"He's very versatile, I know that," Jordan said before the matchup. "And he's their spark plug, so we have to do what we can to contain him."

More than just a spark plug, Penny was the engine that powered the Magic to a 94-88 victory. And despite a pre-game strategy that focused on containing Penny, none of Jordan's and his teammates' defensive techniques slowed him down.

Hardaway burned the Bulls for 36 points, five rebounds and four steals. More importantly, he hit 12 of 18 shots, many of them playing straight up against Jordan. He drove around him and hit jumpers in his face during a performance pitting the old king of the NBA against the new king.

Hardaway also demonstrated his defensive prowess by limiting his counterpart to just five second-half points and none in the last six minutes of the game.

For Michael, it was like looking into a mirror.

Jordan saluted Hardaway after the game, saying, "He is playing with a lot of poise and confidence."

It's the same poise and confidence that has made Jordan the game's greatest player. Perhaps it's contagious.

GARY PAYTON

Penny Hardaway demonstrated a new dimension to his game to Gary Payton during the 1996 Summer Olympics in Atlanta. And Penny didn't even have a basketball in his hands.

It was a dimension that most fans and players may have overlooked, but not Payton.

"The thing I noticed about Penny during all this [the Olympic competition] is how he handled himself after hearing that Shaquille left the Magic," says Payton, the Seattle SuperSonics' All-Star point guard. I know that if Shawn [Kemp, Payton's Seattle teammate] had left me the way Shaquille left Penny, I'd have a breakdown or something. But Penny told Shaq 'congratulations' and wished him the best."

It may not have been the easiest thing for Hardaway to do, but Payton says he handled it like a pro.

As for the Orlando guard's future, Payton believes Hardaway will deliver under the suffocating pressure of being the Magic's No. 1 go-to guy.

"He knows that this is his team now and I think he'll step up and do the job. He'll do great things in Orlando and the Orlando Magic organization will see that," Payton predicts. "The Magic's season all hinges on what Penny will do. I really think Penny is looking forward to the challenge."

Hardaway has talked about his desire to play small forward for the Magic next season. That's fine with Payton, who has had to guard him at least twice in each of the last three seasons. Payton, named the Defensive Player of the Year last season, gives up three inches to Hardaway and always has his work cut out for him when the two match up at point guard.

"He's just a great, great talent. He can do everything . . . like Scottie Pippen," Payton says. "He's just so versatile. The Magic, I think, are at their best when they've got Brian Shaw at the point and then let Penny play shooting guard or small forward. I know that it's tough on him when somebody like me or Mookie [Blaylock] pressure him all night and wear him down.

"But when Penny sets his mind on something and wants to do it, there's no stopping him."

Not even if you're Gary Payton, one of the league's top defensive players.

Gary Payton is convinced that Penny will rise to the challenge of being the No. 1 go-to guy in Orlando following Shaquille O'Neal's move to Los Angeles.

There's no denying it. Penny Hardaway rises to the occasion when it comes to the playoffs. Reggie Miller can give a first-hand testimony of it following their hard-fought playoff battles in two of the last three seasons.

REGGIE MILLER

Reggie Miller believes the free-agent loss of Shaquille O'Neal clears the way for Penny Hardaway to step out of Shaq's immense shadow and into a Jordanesque limelight.

"I think Penny will be the leader of the Orlando team," says Miller, the All-Star guard of the Indiana Pacers. "I think he was the leader even when Shaquille was there."

With O'Neal in Los Angeles, Miller says Hardaway's productivity with the Magic should increase even more.

"He'll raise his level of play, no question, and make everybody else on the team raise their level — Nick Anderson, Dennis Scott. That's the kind of player Penny is," Miller says. "All of them will have to do more because with Shaq, teams had to double down on him and that left Penny one-on-one a lot of times. Now, they don't have to do that."

Miller got a first-hand look at Hardaway under pressure during the first round of the 1994 NBA playoffs. Hardaway, just a rookie, played like a seasoned veteran against Miller's Pacers.

Although Indiana swept the Magic, Hardaway averaged 18.7 points, 6.7 rebounds and seven assists per game.

In the '95 playoffs, Hardaway and the Magic avenged their embarrassing sweep of the previous season by knocking out the Pacers in the Eastern Conference Finals. Because of those experiences with Hardaway, Miller knew the Magic guard was an exceptional player. But the gathering of the Dream Team only made him appreciate Penny more.

"Seeing him all the time with the Dream Team, you see how great a player he is. Because he's 6-8, he can see the floor well. Everybody knows that. But what I've seen is what a great passer he is in traffic," Miller says.

"He's a player, period," Miller continues. "It's hard to say that he's just a point guard. He can play the '1' [point guard], the '2' [shooting guard] and the '3' [small forward]. He plays everything. I wouldn't label him." •

Brian Schmitz is a columnist for The Orlando Sentinel.

Penny Arcade

From his high school days to his All-Star ways, Penny's photogenic image has developed a gallery of portraits

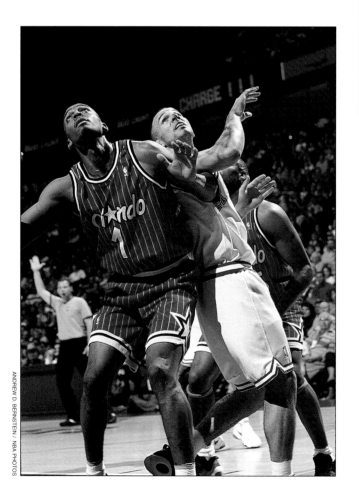

Inside the Paint

Penny's size and leaping ability allow him to venture where shot-blocking centers are mean and point guards are scared — in the paint. Whether he's posting up or dunking, Penny's no outsider to the lane.

High School Daze

Even when Penny really was li'l, he came up huge. His legendary exploits at Treadwell High School in Memphis made headlines and filled gyms, and all of Tennessee soon knew his name.

Making a Point

No matter what jersey he's wearing, Penny's leadership abilities as a point guard set into motion another assault at the basket. With or without Shaquille O'Neal, Penny fills the role of catalyst for the Magic.

Winning Smile

As shiny as a brand new one-cent coin, Penny's winsome smile shows up often whether he is on the court or away from it. Opponents beware: Those pearly whites of his may look friendly, but they shine brightest after a rim-hanging, in-your-face dunk.

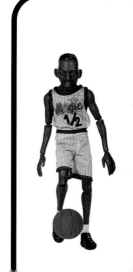

96 ANFERNEE HARDAWAY

Hometown Hero

Penny's decision to play college basketball at Memphis State had the whole town rockin'. The Pyramid arena became the place to be to watch Penny lift the Tigers to national prominence.

Magic
MAN

Penny Hardaway's on-court success and Hall of Fame
potential have worked magic in the basketball card hobby

By Tol Broome

hree years ago the Orlando Magic shocked the NBA and basketball card hobby by trading away No. 1 pick Chris Webber to Golden State for an unproven talent named Anfernee Hardaway. Sure, the Magic also received the Warriors' top draft picks in the 1996, 1998 and 2000 drafts in the deal. But what were they thinking about in passing up a chance to pair the previous year's top pick, Shaquille O'Neal, with former Fab Fiver Webber?

Hobbyists wondered if the Memphis State product had the skills to make a mark with the Magic. They soon found out. When he was named MVP of the Schick Rookie Game during All-Star Weekend festivities, collectors began to see that this Penny was a money player.

Topps spokesman, Marty Appel, says that Hardaway's star appeal in the hobby was evident from the moment he first put on his Orlando jersey. "The NBA has had a remarkable gift for developing star-studded rookie each season to perpetuate excitement that started with Magic and Bird," he says. "Penny Hardaway meets the league's criteria. He has definitely become a go-to-guy for card collectors."

Hardaway's hobby star has continued to rise as accolade upon accolade has been heaped on the shoulders of the 6-8 versatile guard. Many have proclaimed him the Air Apparent to Michael Jordan, who has done nothing to discourage the comparison. The Bulls' living legend has been quoted as saying that Hardaway is the player who most reminds Jordan of himself among today's young

superstars.

While comparisons to His Airness are flattering, another Hardaway backer may carry even more weight. Penny's most outspoken fan has gone along way toward generating excitement for Hardaway. Lil' Penny, Anfernee's alter-ego and Nike shoe commercial sidekick has helped boost Penny's visibility and popularity. There's nothing like a catchy high-profile ad campaign to grab the attention of fans and collectors.

Thanks in part to his alter ego, Li'l Penny, Hardaway is on top of the hobby heap.

During his first three NBA seasons, Hardaway has appeared on many cardboard collectibles. From Day One, hoops hobbyists have hotly pursued Hardaway rookie releases such as his 1993-94 Finest (#189), 1993-94 SkyBox (#259) and 1993-94 Upper Deck SE Electric Gold (#188). Not surprisingly, Penny's most sought after first-year issue is his 1993-94 Finest Refractor (#189), which trails only the Michael Jordan Refractor from the same year for high honors in price.

DOUG WILLIAMS

Appel says that Hardaway is one of the first 10 names that comes up in insert set discussions. He attributes Hardaway's popularity to a combination of factors that include his catchy nickname, a positive image and his smooth all-around on-court skills. His cards have been among the headliners in such insert sets as 1994-95 Upper Deck Special Edition Gold (#63), 1995-96 Finest Hot Stuff (#4), 1995-96 Fleer Metal Molten Metal (#1) and 1995-96 SP Holoview Die Cuts (#24) just to name a few.

In fact, Hardaway's hobby popularity has not stopped with his inclusion in as many insert sets as the league will allow. Upper Deck recently signed Penny to an endorsement deal that will headline Hardaway as the lead pitchman for Upper Deck basketball releases in 1996-97. Upper Deck basketball product manager Rick Schwartz reports Hardaway's first order of business as Upper Deck's lead spokesman was to autograph an unreported but "very limited" number of autographed insert cards for the 1996 SP^X release. Hardaway will also play a prominent role in card sets produced to honor the Olympic team. Hardaway's card checklist has swelled a great deal with the release of such 1996 USA Basketball insert cards as SkyBox (#1) and Ultra (#1), as well as multiple appearances in separate USA sets issued by Fleer, SkyBox and Upper Deck.

Appel, however, isn't sure that the Olympic experience had nearly as much hobby impact as was evident in 1992.

"No one really seemed to rise in stature this year from an Olympic appearance," explains Appel. "All of the players, including Hardaway, lost nothing by playing but they all seemed to gain little in terms of added hobby appeal this time."

One major hobby event that did occur during the Olympics was the signing of O'Neal by the Lakers to a $120 million free agent contract. While the signing removes Hardaway from Shaq's very large shadow as Orlando's most visible player, it raises questions. Can the Magic still contend for an NBA title without O'Neal? Will Hardaway be able to elevate his game for a full season as he did during the 25 games Shaq was injured last season?

Dealer Andy Stoltz of A&S Sports Memorabilia in Tampa doesn't expect any negative repercussions from Shaq's departure on Hardaway's hobby appeal.

"Even with Shaq in Orlando last year, Hardaway still outsold O'Neal two to one in our shop," says Stolz, who sells memorabilia as well as cards. "Hardaway was close to Jordan last year in terms of basketball card popularity."

Stolz says that all Hardaway cards are popular items in the area.

"All of the price levels move well for Hardaway cards," he explains. "Kids buy the lower priced cards and adults buy up the high-end stuff. I think Hardaway could be the next Jordan in the hobby on a long-term basis."

Schwartz agrees with Stoltz that O'Neal's departure will increase Hardaway's hobby popularity.

"Shaq leaving elevates Penny's position in the hobby," Schwartz says. "He's the main man now in Orlando. He can carry a team for an extended period of time just like he carried Orlando last year when O'Neal was out with his thumb injury."

Fleer/SkyBox spokesman Rich Bradley believes that the jury is still out on the true impact of O'Neals' departure on Hardaway's hobby appeal.

"Shaq's signing with the Lakers will help and hurt Hardaway at the same time," Bradley says. "On the one hand, he was in Shaq's shadow and now it will

be Penny's show. But without Shaq there, not as much attention will be on the Magic."

Bradley says that hobbyists can expect to see more insert cards of Hardaway in 1996-97 because of league limitations that sometimes prevent card companies from including more than one player from the same team in an insert set. But Bradley isn't convinced collectors will be more interested in chasing Hardaway's chase cards.

"The 1996-97 season will be the determining year for Hardaway," Bradley says. "Will he take the Magic further than they have been in the past or will he become the next Larry Johnson. Johnson was supposed to be the player to take the Hornets to the Promised Land but he didn't deliver.

"Shaq's departure definitely puts the hobby spotlight more on Hardaway," continues Bradley. "We will find out if he is up to the task. It is difficult for a guard to carry a team in the NBA. Yes, there is a guy in Chicago who has. But we may just find out with O'Neal's departure if Hardaway really will be the one to take over when Jordan retires for good."

If Hardaway's NBA prowess during his first three years in the league is any indication, then he should prove capable of stepping up his game to another level. And while it remains to be seen if he is the hobby's next Jordan, Hardaway's rare all-around on-court skill level and nice guy off-court image should continue to provide Penny's from heaven for Hardaway hobbyist who continue in hot pursuit of his cards. •

Tol Broome is a freelance writer in Greensboro, N.C.

Penny Hardaway's

Comprehensive Card Checklist and Price Guide

- ❏ 1992-96 Sports Illustrated for Kids (#279) $8
- ❏ 1992-93 Memphis State #4 $15
- ❏ 1993 Classic Deathwatch Jumbos #SE3 $15
- ❏ 1993 Classic Draft #2 $2.50
- ❏ 1993 Classic Draft Acetate Stars #AD1 $16

1993-94 Fleer First Year Phenoms #2

- ❏ 1993 Classic Draft Chromium Stars #DS37 $5
- ❏ 1993 Classic Draft Draft Day #1 $8
- ❏ 1993 Classic Draft Draft Day #2 $8
- ❏ 1993 Classic Draft Draft Day #3 $8

- ❏ 1993 Classic Draft Illustrated #SS3 $12
- ❏ 1993 Classic Draft LPs #LP2 $12
- ❏ 1993 Classic Draft Previews #BK3 $30
- ❏ 1993 Classic Draft Special Bonus #SB2 $5
- ❏ 1993 Classic Four-Sport #2 $2
- ❏ 1993 Classic Four-Sport #313 $.60
- ❏ 1993 Classic Four-Sport Acetates #2 $10
- ❏ 1993 Classic Four-Sport Chromium Draft #DS42 $4
- ❏ 1993 Classic Four-Sport LPs #LP3 $10
- ❏ 1993 Classic Four-Sport Power Pick Bonus #PP2 $4
- ❏ 1993 Classic Four Sport Tri-Cards #TC1 $12
- ❏ 1993 Classic Futures #3 $4
- ❏ 1993 Classic Futures LPs #LP2 $10
- ❏ 1993 Classic Futures Team #2 $12
- ❏ 1993 Classic McDonald's Four-Sport #21 $3

- ❏ 1993-94 Finest #189 $30
- ❏ 1993-94 Finest Refractors #189 $400
- ❏ 1993-94 Fleer #343 $5
- ❏ 1993-94 Fleer First Year Phenoms #2 $6
- ❏ 1993-94 Fleer Lottery Exchange #3 $15

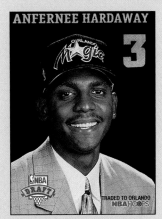

1993-94 Hoops Draft Redemption #LP3

- ❏ 1993-94 Hoops #380 $5
- ❏ 1993-94 Hoops Gold #380 $10
- ❏ 1993-94 Hoops Draft Redemption #LP3 $30
- ❏ 1993-94 Hoops Magic's All-Rookies #3 $40
- ❏ 1993-94 Jam Session #159 $10

- ❏ 1993-94 Jam Session Rookie Standouts #4 $15
- ❏ 1993 Memphis Police (NNO) $5
- ❏ 1993-94 SkyBox #259 $6
- ❏ 1993-94 SkyBox #310 $1.50
- ❏ 1993-94 SkyBox Draft Picks #3 $30
- ❏ 1993-94 SkyBox Thunder and Lightning #TL6 $20
- ❏ 1993-94 SkyBox Schick #20 $25
- ❏ 1993-94 Stadium Club #266 $2.50
- ❏ 1993-94 Stadium Club #308 $6
- ❏ 1993-94 Stadium Club First Day Issue #266 $90
- ❏ 1993-94 Stadium Club First Day Issue #308 $225
- ❏ 1993-94 Stadium Club Beam Team #23 $50
- ❏ 1993-94 Stadium Club Super Teams NBA Finals #266 $6
- ❏ 1993-94 Stadium Club Super Teams NBA Finals

#308 $15

❏ 1993-94 Stadium
Club Members Only
#266 $8

❏ 1993-94 Stadium
Club Members Only
#308 $20

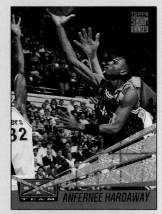

**1993-94 Stadium Club
Beam Team #23**

❏ 1993-94 Stadium
Club Members Only
#BT23 $20

❏ 1993-94 Stadium
Club Members Only
59 #4 $6

❏ 1993-94 Topps
#334 $5

❏ 1993-94 Topps Gold
#334G $12

❏ 1993-94 Topps Black
Gold #19 $15

❏ 1993-94 Ultra
#305 $6

❏ 1993-94 Ultra All-
Rookie Series #4 $25

❏ 1993-94 Ultra Famous
Nicknames #5 $25

❏ 1993-94 Upper Deck
#382 $6

❏ 1993-94 Upper Deck
#484 $2.50

❏ 1993-94 Upper Deck

Rookie Exchange
#RE3 $6

❏ 1993-94 Upper Deck
Rookie Exchange Gold
#RE3 $12

❏ 1993-94 Upper Deck
Rookie Standouts
#RS17 $25

❏ 1993-94 Upper Deck
Holojams #H30 $8

❏ 1993-94 Upper Deck
Wal-Mart Jumbos
#382 $15

❏ 1993-94 Upper Deck
Pro View #83 $6

❏ 1993-94 Upper Deck
SE #51 $6

❏ 1993-94 Upper Deck
SE #188 $2.50

❏ 1993-94 Upper Deck
SE #217 $1.50

❏ 1993-94 Upper Deck
SE Electric Court
#51 $12

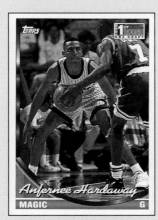

1993-94 Topps #334

❏ 1993-94 Upper Deck
SE Electric Court
#188 $5

❏ 1993-94 Upper Deck
SE Electric Court
#217 $3

❏ 1993-94 Upper Deck
SE Electric Gold

#51 $125

❏ 1993-94 Upper Deck
SE Electric Gold
#188 $50

❏ 1993-94 Upper Deck
SE Electric Gold
#217 $30

❏ 1993-94 Upper Deck
SE Die Cut All-Stars
#E12 $200

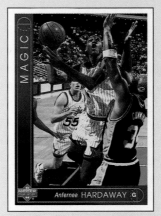

**1993-94 Upper Deck
#382**

❏ 1994 Classic C3*
#2 $5

❏ 1994 Classic Draft
#14 $.25

❏ 1994 Classic Draft
Gold #14 $1

❏ 1994 Classic Images *
#6 $2

❏ 1994 Classic Images *
#134 $.60

❏ 1994 Classic Images
Chrome * #CC2 $15

❏ 1994 Classic Images
Sudden Impact *
#SI13 $2

❏ 1994 Kenner Starting
Lineup #10 $60

❏ 1994 Pacific Prism
Draft Samples #3 $6

❏ 1994 Pacific Prism

Draft #21 $2.50

❏ 1994 Pacific Prism
Draft #69 $2.50

❏ 1994 Pacific Prism
Gold #21 $12

❏ 1994 Pacific Prism
Gold #69 $12

❏ 1994 SkyBox Blue
Chips #16 $.25

❏ 1994 SkyBox Blue
Chips #29 $.25

❏ 1994 SkyBox Blue
Chips #34 $.25

❏ 1994 SkyBox Blue
Chips #44 $.25

❏ 1994 SkyBox Blue
Chips #56 $.50

❏ 1994 SkyBox Blue
Chips #67 $.25

❏ 1994 SkyBox Blue
Chips #82 $.25

❏ 1994 SkyBox Blue
Chips #85 $.50

❏ 1994 SkyBox Blue
Chips Foil #F1 $12

❏ 1994 SkyBox Blue
Chips Foil #F2 $12

❏ 1994 Upper Deck
European French
#138 $15

❏ 1994 Upper Deck

European German
#138 $18

❏ 1994 Upper Deck
European Italian
#138 $12

❏ 1994 Upper Deck
European Spanish
#138 $10

**1993-94 Upper Deck
Pro View #83**

❏ 1994-95 Classic Assets
* #53 $1

❏ 1994-95 Classic Assets
* #78 $1

❏ 1994-95 Classic Assets
Silver Signature *
#27 $6

❏ 1994-95 Classic Assets
Phone Cards $50
#2 $150

❏ 1994-95 Classic Assets
Phone Cards One
Minute #31 $6

❏ 1994-95 Collector's
Choice #1 $1.50

❏ 1994-95 Collector's
Choice Silver Sig-
nature #1 $4

❏ 1994-95 Collector's
Choice Gold Signature
#1 $50

❏ 1994-95 Collector's
Choice Crash the

Game Assists
#A6 $10

❏ 1994-95 Collector's
Choice Crash the
Game Assists Ex-
change #A6 $5

❏ 1994-95 Embossed
#68 $3

❏ 1994-95 Embossed
Golden Idols #68 $8

❏ 1994-95 Emotion
#69 $4

❏ 1994-95 Emotion
#111 $2

❏ 1994-95 Emotion
X-Cited #X2 $15

❏ 1994-95 Finest
#167 $8

❏ 1994-95 Finest
Refractors
#167 $400

❏ 1994-95 Finest
Cornerstone
#CS12 $40

❏ 1994-95 Finest Iron
Men #7 $20

❏ 1994-95 Finest Lottery
Prize #LP20 $15

❏ 1994-95 Finest
Marathon Men
#10 $40

❏ 1994-95 Flair #106 $6

❏ 1994-95 Flair Hot
Numbers #4 $15

❏ 1994-95 Flair
Playmakers #4 $8

❏ 1994-95 Fleer
#159 $1.50

❏ 1994-95 Fleer Pro-
Visions #8 $2.50

❏ 1994-95 Fleer
Rookie Sensations
#9 $12

❏ 1994-95 Fleer Young
Lions #2 $5

❏ 1994-95 Hoops
#151 $1.50

❏ 1994-95 Hoops
#264 $.75

❏ 1994-95 Hoops
#423 $1

❏ 1994-95 Hoops Big
Numbers #BN8 $20

**1994-95 Collector's
Choice #1**

❏ 1994-95 Hoops Big
Numbers Rainbow
#BN8 $20

❏ 1994-95 Hoops Power
Ratings #PR38 $3

❏ 1994-95 Hoops
Supreme Court
#SC32 $5

❏ 1994-95 Hoops Sheets
#11 $5

❏ 1994-95 Jam Session
#135 $3

❏ 1994-95 Jam Session
Flashing Stars
#1 $5

❏ 1994-95 Jam Session
Second Year Stars
#2 $5

❏ 1994-95 Panini
#96 $4

❏ 1994-95 Panini
#B $4

❏ 1994-95 Pro Mags
#92 $10

❏ 1994-95 SkyBox
#117 $2.50

❏ 1994-95 SkyBox
#186 $.40

❏ 1994-95 SkyBox
Center Stage
#CS3 $40

❏ 1994-95 SkyBox
Ragin' Rookies
#RR18 $15

❏ 1994-95 SkyBox
SkyTech Force
#SF6 $4

❏ 1994-95 SP #122 $4

❏ 1994-95 SP Die-Cuts
#D122 $10

❏ 1994-95 SP
Championship
#102 $2.50

**1994-95 Finest Lottery
Prize #LP20**

❏ 1994-95 SP
Championship Die
Cuts #102 $6

❏ 1994-95 SP
Championship Future
Playoff Heroes
#F2 $15

❏ 1994-95 SP

Championship Future Playoff Heroes Die Cuts #F2 $90

❏ 1994-95 Stadium Club #16 $2.50

❏ 1994-95 Stadium Club #17 $1.25

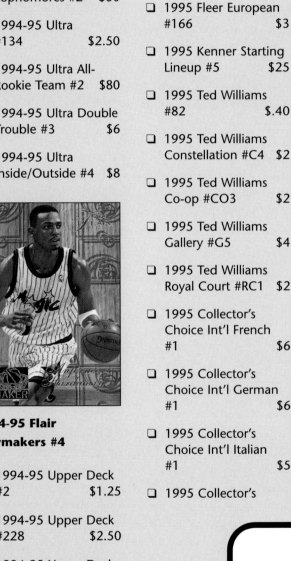

1994-95 Flair #106

❏ 1994-95 Stadium Club #279 $.60

❏ 1994-95 Stadium Club First Day Issue #16 $80

❏ 1994-95 Stadium Club First Day Issue #17 $40

❏ 1994-95 Stadium Club First Day Issue #279 $20

❏ 1994-95 Stadium Club Dynasty and Destiny #3B $4

❏ 1994-95 Stadium Club Rising Stars #10 $30

❏ 1994-95 Stadium Club Super Teams Division Winners #M16 $6

❏ 1994-95 Stadium Club Super Teams Master Photos #M8 $8

❏ 1994-95 Stadium Club Super Teams NBA Finals #16 $6

❏ 1994-95 Stadium Club Super Teams NBA Finals #17 $3

❏ 1994-95 Stadium Club Super Teams NBA Finals #279 $1.50

❏ 1994-95 Stadium Club Team of the Future #1 $12

❏ 1994-95 Stadium Club Members Only #16 $5

❏ 1994-95 Stadium Club Members Only #17 $2.50

❏ 1994-95 Stadium Club Members Only #279 $1.50

❏ 1994-95 Stadium Club Members Only #DD3B $2.50

❏ 1994-95 Stadium Club Members Only #RS10 $10

❏ 1994-95 Stadium Club Members Only #TF1 $5

❏ 1994-95 Stadium Club Members Only 50 #7 $2

❏ 1994-95 Topps #14 $.75

❏ 1994-95 Topps #75 $1.50

❏ 1994-95 Topps #76 $.75

❏ 1994-95 Topps Spectralight #14 $8

❏ 1994-95 Topps Spectralight #75 $15

❏ 1994-95 Topps Spectralight #76 $8

❏ 1994-95 Topps Franchise/Futures #18 $20

❏ 1994-95 Topps Own the Game #13 $4

❏ 1994-95 Topps Super Sophomores #2 $30

❏ 1994-95 Ultra #134 $2.50

❏ 1994-95 Ultra All-Rookie Team #2 $80

❏ 1994-95 Ultra Double Trouble #3 $6

❏ 1994-95 Ultra Inside/Outside #4 $8

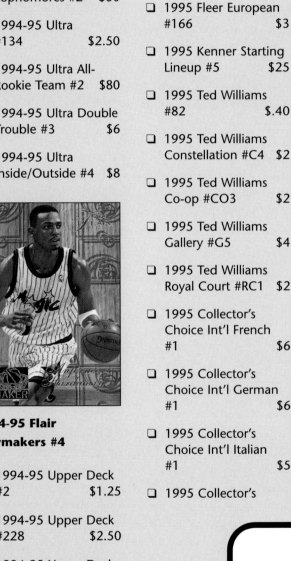

1994-95 Flair Playmakers #4

❏ 1994-95 Upper Deck #2 $1.25

❏ 1994-95 Upper Deck #228 $2.50

❏ 1994-95 Upper Deck Predictor League Leaders #R17 $12

❏ 1994-95 Upper Deck Predictor League Leaders Redemption #R17 $6

❏ 1994-95 Upper Deck Special Edition #63 $5

❏ 1994-95 Upper Deck Special Edition Gold #63 $40

❏ 1994-95 Upper Deck Sheets #1 $10

❏ 1994-95 Upper Deck Sheets #2 $8

❏ 1995 Fleer European #166 $3

❏ 1995 Kenner Starting Lineup #5 $25

❏ 1995 Ted Williams #82 $.40

❏ 1995 Ted Williams Constellation #C4 $2

❏ 1995 Ted Williams Co-op #CO3 $2

❏ 1995 Ted Williams Gallery #G5 $4

❏ 1995 Ted Williams Royal Court #RC1 $2

❏ 1995 Collector's Choice Int'l French #1 $6

❏ 1995 Collector's Choice Int'l German #1 $6

❏ 1995 Collector's Choice Int'l Italian #1 $5

❏ 1995 Collector's

Choice Int'l Japanese
#1 $6

❑ 1995 Collector's
Choice Int'l Spanish
#1 $4

❑ 1995-96 Collector's
Choice #145 $1.50

❑ 1995-96 Collector's
Choice #384 $.75

❑ 1995-96 Collector's
Choice #399 $.75

**1994-95 SP
Championship Future
Playoff Heroes #F2**

❑ 1995-96 Collector's
Choice Retail Jumbo
(#399) $5

❑ 1995-96 Collector's
Choice Player's Club
#145 $4

❑ 1995-96 Collector's
Choice Player's Club
#384 $2

❑ 1995-96 Collector's
Choice Player's Club
#399 $2

❑ 1995-96 Collector's
Choice Player's
Club Platinum
#145 $40

❑ 1995-96 Collector's
Choice Player's Club
Platinum #384 $20

❑ 1995-96 Collector's
Choice Player's Club
Platinum #399 $20

❑ 1995-96 Collector's
Choice Crash
Assists/Reb. Silver
#C15A $4

❑ 1995-96 Collector's
Choice Crash
Assists/Reb. Silver
#C15B $4

❑ 1995-96 Collector's
Choice Crash
Assists/Reb. Silver
#C15C $4

❑ 1995-96 Collector's
Choice Crash
Assists/Reb. Silver
Exchange
#C15 $2

❑ 1995-96 Collector's
Choice Crash
Assists/Reb. Gold
#C15A $15

❑ 1995-96 Collector's
Choice Crash
Assists/Reb. Gold
#C15B $15

❑ 1995-96 Collector's
Choice Crash
Assists/Reb. Gold
#C15C $15

❑ 1995-96 Collector's
Choice Crash
Assists/Reb. Gold
Exchange
#C15 $8

❑ 1995-96 Collector's
Choice Crash Scoring
Silver #C5A $4

❑ 1995-96 Collector's
Choice Crash Scoring
Silver #C5B $4

❑ 1995-96 Collector's
Choice Crash Scoring
Silver #C5C $4

❑ 1995-96 Collector's

Choice Crash Scoring
Silver Exchange
#C5 $2

❑ 1995-96 Collector's
Choice Crash Scoring
Gold #C5A $15

❑ 1995-96 Collector's
Choice Crash Scoring
Gold #C5B $15

❑ 1995-96 Collector's
Choice Crash Scoring
Gold #C5C $15

**1994-95 Topps Super
Sophomores #2**

❑ 1995-96 Collector's
Choice Crash Scoring
Gold Exchange
#C5 $8

❑ 1995-96 Finest
#234 $8

❑ 1995-96 Finest
Refractors
#234 $225

❑ 1995-96 Finest Dish
and Swish
#DS19 $125

❑ 1995-96 Finest Hot
Stuff #HS4 $20

❑ 1995-96 Finest
Mystery #M3 $6

❑ 1995-96 Finest
Mystery
Borderless/Silver
#M3 $30

❑ 1995-96 Finest
Mystery Borderless
Refractors/Gold
#M3 $350

❑ 1995-96 Flair #96 $6

❑ 1995-96 Flair #232 $2

❑ 1995-96 Flair New
Heights #1 $30

❑ 1995-96 Flair
Perimeter Power
#3 $12

❑ 1995-96 Flair Play
Makers #2 $125

❑ 1995-96 Fleer
#129 $1.50

❑ 1995-96 Fleer All-Stars
#4 $1.50

❑ 1995-96 Fleer End to
End #6 $5

❑ 1995-96 Fleer
Franchise Futures
#2 $20

**1994-95 Upper Deck
All-Rookie Team #2**

❑ 1995-96 Fleer Metal
#77 $3

❑ 1995-96 Fleer Metal
#209 $1.25

❑ 1995-96 Fleer Metal
Silver Spotlight
#77 $9

❑ 1995-96 Fleer Metal

Molten Metal
#1 $75

❑ 1995-96 Fleer Metal
Scoring Magnets
#1 $50

❑ 1995-96 Fleer Metal
Slick Silver #2 $12

❑ 1995-96 Hoop
Magazine/Mother's
Cookies #19 $10

❑ 1995-96 Hoops
#116 $1.50

❑ 1995-96 Hoops
#394 $.75

❑ 1995-96 Hoops
HoopStars #HS8 $8

❑ 1995-96 Hoops
Number Crunchers
#6 $2.50

❑ 1995-96 Hoops Power
Palette #7 $20

❑ 1995-96 Hoops
SkyView #SV7 $100

❑ 1995-96 Hoops Top
Ten #AR5 $10

❑ 1995-96 Jam Session
#76 $2.50

❑ 1995-96 Jam Session
Die Cuts #76 $6

❑ 1995-96 Jam Session
Show Stoppers
#1 $40

❑ 1995-96 Panini
#39 $2.50

❑ 1995-96 Pro Mags
#91 $6

❑ 1995-96 Pro Mags
Die Cuts #5 $6

❑ 1995-96 Pro Mags
USA Basketball
#8 $6

❑ 1995-96 SkyBox
#88 $2

❑ 1995-96 SkyBox
#292 $1

❑ 1995-96 SkyBox
Atomic #A15 $5

❑ 1995-96 SkyBox Hot
Sparks #HS6 $12

❑ 1995-96 SkyBox
Standouts #S7 $20

❑ 1995-96 SkyBox USA
Basketball #U1 $10

❑ 1995-96 SkyBox E-XL
#59 $4

❑ 1995-96 SkyBox E-XL
Blue #59 $10

❑ 1995-96 SkyBox E-XL
Natural Born Thrillers
#6 $60

**1994-95 Upper Deck
Predictor League
Leaders #R17**

❑ 1995-96 SkyBox E-XL
No Boundaries #7 $30

❑ 1995-96 SP #95 $3

❑ 1995-96 SP All-Stars
#AS1 $12

❑ 1995-96 SP All-Stars
Gold #AS1 $100

❑ 1995-96 SP Holoviews
#PC24 $20

❑ 1995-96 SP
Holoview Die Cuts
#PC24 $200

❑ 1995-96 SP
Championship
#75 $2.50

❑ 1995-96 SP
Championship
#136 $1.25

❑ 1995-96 SP
Championship
Championship Shots
#S4 $5

❑ 1995-96 SP
Championship
Championship Shots
Gold #S4 $50

❑ 1995-96 Stadium
Club #32 $2.50

❑ 1995-96 Stadium
Club Nemeses
#N7 $15

❑ 1995-96 Stadium
Club Warp Speed
#WS4 $30

❑ 1995-96 Stadium
Club Wizards
#W10 $30

❑ 1995-96 Stadium
Club Members Only
#32 $4

❑ 1995-96 Stadium
Club Members Only
#N7 $6

❑ 1995-96 Stadium
Club Members Only
#WS4 $8

❑ 1995-96 Stadium
Club Members Only
#W10 $8

❑ 1995-96 Topps
#155 $1.50

❑ 1995-96 Topps
Mystery Finest
#M2 $25

❑ 1995-96 Topps
Mystery Finest
Refractors
#M2 $90

❑ 1995-96 Topps Show
Stoppers #SS4 $20

❑ 1995-96 Topps Spark
Plugs #SP4 $8

❑ 1995-96 Topps Top
Flight #TF9 $20

**1995-96 Collector's
Choice Crash the Game
Assists/Rebounds #C15**

❑ 1995-96 Topps Whiz
Kids #WK9 $20

❑ 1995-96 Topps World
Class #WC7 $10

❑ 1995-96 Topps Gallery
#19 $3

❑ 1995-96 Topps
Gallery Players
Private Issue
#19 $50

❑ 1995-96 Topps Gallery
Photo Gallery
#PG13 $30

❏ 1995-96 Ultra
#125 $2.50

❏ 1995-96 Ultra
#310 $1.25

❏ 1995-96 Ultra Gold
Medallion #125 $15

❏ 1995-96 Ultra All-NBA
#1 $6

❏ 1995-96 Ultra All-NBA
Gold Medallion
#1 $18

1995-96 Finest #234

❏ 1995-96 Ultra Double
Trouble #2 $4

❏ 1995-96 Ultra Double
Trouble Gold
Medallion #2 $12

❏ 1995-96 Ultra Rising
Stars #2 $40

❏ 1995-96 Ultra Rising
Stars Gold Medallion
#2 $120

❏ 1995-96 Ultra USA
Basketball #1 $60

❏ 1995-96 Upper Deck
#170 $1.25

❏ 1995-96 Upper Deck
#277 $2.50

❏ 1995-96 Upper Deck
#316 $1.25

❏ 1995-96 Upper Deck

Retail Jumbo
(#170) $5

❏ 1995-96 Upper Deck
Retail Jumbo
(#316) $5

❏ 1995-96 Upper Deck
Electric Court #170 $3

❏ 1995-96 Upper Deck
Electric Court #277 $6

❏ 1995-96 Upper Deck
Electric Court #316 $3

❏ 1995-96 Upper Deck
Electric Court Gold
#170 $30

❏ 1995-96 Upper Deck
Electric Court Gold
#277 $60

❏ 1995-96 Upper Deck
Electric Court Gold
#316 $30

❏ 1995-96 Upper Deck
All-Star Class
#AS1 $30

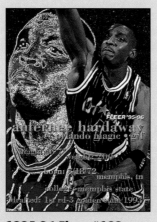

1995-96 Fleer #129

❏ 1995-96 Upper Deck
Predictor MVP
#R9 $8

❏ 1995-96 Upper Deck
Predictor MVP
Exchange #R9 $4

❏ 1995-96 Upper Deck
Predictor Player of the
Week #H6 $10

❏ 1995-96 Upper Deck
Predictor Player of the
Week Exchange
#H6 $4

❏ 1995-96 Upper Deck
Special Edition
#60 $8

❏ 1995-96 Upper Deck
Special Edition Gold
#60 $60

❏ 1996 Collector's
Choice Int'l French I
#145 $4

❏ 1996 Collector's
Choice Int'l French II
#174 $2

❏ 1996 Collector's
Choice Int'l French II
#189 $2

❏ 1996 Collector's
Choice Int'l German I
#145 $4

❏ 1996 Collector's
Choice Int'l German II
#174 $2

❏ 1996 Collector's
Choice Int'l German II
#189 $2

❏ 1996 Collector's
Choice Int'l Italian I
#145 $4

❏ 1996 Collector's
Choice Int'l Italian II
#174 $2

❏ 1996 Collector's
Choice Int'l Italian II
#189 $2

❏ 1996 Collector's
Choice Int'l Japanese
#145 $4

❏ 1996 Collector's
Choice Int'l Japanese
#384 $2

❏ 1996 Collector's
Choice Int'l Japanese
#399 $2

❏ 1996 Collector's
Choice Int'l Latin I
#145 $4

❏ 1996 Collector's
Choice Int'l Latin II
#174 $2

❏ 1996 Collector's
Choice Int'l Latin II
#189 $2

1995-96 SP #95

❏ 1996 Collector's
Choice Int'l Northern
Europe I #145 $4

❏ 1996 Collector's
Choice Int'l Northern
Europe II #174 $2

❏ 1996 Collector's
Choice Int'l Northern
Europe II #189 $2

❏ 1996 Collector's
Choice Int'l Portugese
I #145 $4

❏ 1996 Collector's
Choice Int'l Portugese
II #174 $2

❏ 1996 Collector's
Choice Int'l Portugese
II #189 $2

❏ 1996 Collector's
Choice Int'l Spanish I
#145 $4

❏ 1996 Collector's
Choice Int'l Spanish II
#174 $2

- 1996 Collector's Choice Int'l Spanish II #189 $2
- 1996 Fleer USA #1 $8
- 1996 Fleer USA #11 $2.50
- 1996 Fleer USA #21 $8
- 1996 Fleer USA #31 $2.50
- 1996 Fleer USA #41 $8
- 1996 Fleer USA Heroes #1 $50
- 1996 SkyBox/Texaco USA #2 $3
- 1996 SkyBox USA #1 $1
- 1996 SkyBox USA #11 $1
- 1996 SkyBox USA #21 $1

1995-96 Topps Gallery #19

- 1996 SkyBox USA #31 $1
- 1996 SkyBox USA #41 $1
- 1996 SkyBox USA Bronze #B1 $10
- 1996 SkyBox USA

Bronze Sparkle #B1 $15
- 1996 SkyBox USA Gold #G1 $80
- 1996 SkyBox USA Gold Sparkle #G1 $120

1995-96 Upper Deck #277

- 1996 SkyBox USA #Q1 $4
- 1996 SkyBox USA #Q12 $1
- 1996 SkyBox USA #Q13 $1
- 1996 SkyBox USA Silver #S1 $30
- 1996 SkyBox USA Silver Sparkle #S1 $45
- 1996 SP^x #34 $15
- 1996 SP^x #T1 $25
- 1996 SP^x #NNO $400
- 1996 SP^x Gold #34 $45
- 1996 SP^x Holoview Heroes #H7 $40
- 1996 Upper Deck USA #1 $.75
- 1996 Upper Deck USA #2 $.75

- 1996 Upper Deck USA #3 $.75
- 1996 Upper Deck USA #4 $.75
- 1996 Upper Deck USA #49 $.75
- 1996 Upper Deck USA Anfernee Hardaway American Made #A1 $15
- 1996 Upper Deck USA Anfernee Hardaway American Made #A2 $15
- 1996 Upper Deck USA Anfernee Hardaway American Made #A3 $15
- 1996 Upper Deck USA Anfernee Hardaway American Made #A4 $15

1996 SP^x Tribute Card #T1

- 1996 Upper Deck USA Follow Your Dreams #F1 $5
- 1996 Upper Deck USA Follow Your Dreams Exchange #F1 $5
- 1996 Upper Deck USA SP Career Statistics #S1 $2.50
- 1996 Upper Deck USA

SP Career Statistics Gold #S1 $30
- 1996-97 Fleer #78 $1.50
- 1996-97 Fleer Franchise Futures #2 $35
- 1996-97 Fleer Stackhouse's All-Fleer #2 $6
- 1996-97 Hoops #111 $1.50
- 1996-97 Hoops Head to Head #H6 $20
- 1996-97 Topps #110 $1.50
- 1996-97 Topps NBA at 50 #110 $9
- 1996-97 Topps Hobby Masters #HM6 $30
- 1996-97 Topps Holding Court #HC5 $25
- 1996-97 Topps Holding Court Refractors #HC5 $80

Sources: *Beckett Basketball Monthly #'s73-75 & Beckett Basketball Card Price Guide #5.*

Soaring into
Stardom

The beginning of Anfernee Hardaway's college basketball career was grounded by academic problems and a stray bullet. But as soon as he was cleared for takeoff, Hardaway immediately began entertaining fans and impressing scouts with his high-flying performances. The following pages chart Penny's season-by-season flight pattern.

By Tim Povtak

1991-92

Anfernee Hardaway missed his freshman season because of academic troubles. He later missed summer workouts because he was shot in the foot as a bystander to a robbery attempt in April.

But he didn't miss much after that.

Hardaway shook off the rust quickly and launched a new era at Memphis State University. The Tigers began play in the Great Midwest Conference. They moved to The Pyramid, their new downtown arena. And they quickly learned how good Hardaway really was.

Showing the versatility that would

G	FG-FGA	PCT	FT-FTA	PCT	REB-AVG	AST	PTS-AVG
34	209-483	.433	103-158	.652	237-7.0	188	59-17.4

become his trademark, Hardaway averaged 17.4 points, seven rebounds and 5.5 assists. He was the only player in NCAA Division I to finish among the top five in his conference in points, rebounds, assists, steals and blocked shots.

Not only was Hardaway named conference Newcomer of the Year, he also claimed its Player of the Year honor. Although the team struggled early, Hardaway led the Tigers to a surprisingly strong finish and into the NCAA tournament. The Tigers, seeded sixth in their region, beat Pepperdine, Arkansas and Georgia Tech to reach the Elite Eight, where they lost to Cincinnati.

Penny's first season of college basketball was impressive enough to earn a spot on the USA Developmental Team that trained against the 1992 U.S. Olympic Dream Team. That's where Hardaway got his first close-up look at Michael Jordan, Larry Bird and Magic Johnson, three of the game's all-time

greats. He learned lessons playing against them that he never would forget.

Hardaway's shooting eye was just developing that first season at Memphis State. He made just 65 percent of his free throws and 43 percent of his field-goal attempts. But he quickly started zeroing-in from three-point range. As Penny showcased his talents, the national media took notice. Following the success of his sophomore season, Hardaway earned honorable mention honors on the Associated Press All-America Team.

"The expectations surrounding him were enormous," says Memphis coach Larry Finch. "And he showed quickly what all the fuss was about. You knew from the start, he was going to be a great player."

1992-93

Buoyed by his summer experience against the Olympic Dream Team, Anfernee Hardaway blossomed during his junior season at Memphis State.

His second and final season at MSU was highlighted by one spectacular week in January. Hardaway was on fire as the Tigers beat Georgia State, Vanderbilt and DePaul. The hometown hero averaged 27.3 points, 14 rebounds, 10 assists, 2.7 steals and 1.3 blocked shots, while shooting 55.5 percent from the field.

He recorded the first triple double

Tigers to an upset victory over fourth-ranked Cincinnati. It was the school's 1,000th victory, a much-celebrated milestone.

He rang up 37 points against Brigham Young University and 35 points against DePaul. He led the Tigers to a 20-12 record and another berth in the NCAA tournament. The season ended on a down note, though. Hardaway struggled and the Tigers were upset by Western Kentucky in the first round of the tournament. Coincidentally, that game was played in Orlando, where Hardaway would later reach stardom in

G	FG-FGA	PCT	FT-FTA	PCT	REB-AVG	AST	PTS-AVG
32	249-522	.477	158-206	.767	273-8.5	204	729-22.8

in school history when he posted 21 points, 15 rebounds and 14 assists against Georgia State. Two nights later, he notched another triple double as MSU beat 18th-ranked Vanderbilt. His 26 points, 12 rebounds and 10 assists against the nationally-ranked Commodores raised the eyebrows of some eager NBA scouts.

For the season, Penny averaged 22.8 points, 8.5 rebounds and 6.4 assists and was named first-team All-America by six different organizations. He also was a finalist for the John Wooden Award, given to the nation's top college player.

Hardaway was named conference Player of the Year for the second consecutive season. He took conference Player of the Week honors a record four times. And he set school records with 729 points and 73 three-pointers. Hardaway's versatility allowed him to play every position on the floor.

On Feb. 6, 1993, Hardaway led the

his professional career.

When the season ended, it didn't take him long to decide to leave school. Even though he led the Tigers in grade point average for three semesters, Penny didn't need an economic degree to decide it was time to pursue a professional basketball career.

Hardaway became the No. 3 pick in the 1993 draft by Golden State, which promptly traded him to Orlando, where he would start his NBA career.

1993-94

Orlando Magic fans booed Anfernee Hardaway when the team completed a draft-day trade to obtain him. But it didn't take long for the boos to turn to cheers. After just a few weeks, Magic fans were hooked on their new superstar.

Hardaway began the season at shooting guard, then moved to point guard in February. Although there were times when he looked a little unsure of his new surroundings, he caught on quickly.

Late in the season, Hardaway posted his first NBA triple double with 14 points, 12 assists and 11 rebounds, a hint of the versatility he would deliver often in his young career. Although he finished a close second in Rookie of the Year balloting to Chris Webber (the player he was traded for), he was the Most Valuable Player in the NBA Rookie Game at the All-Star Weekend.

Penny may have looked almost frail at 190 pounds, but he was durable, playing through a variety of nagging injuries that would have worn down a less-competitive person. He was the only rookie in the league to start all 82 regular season games.

He played 49 minutes in one game at Boston, scored 38 points at Charlotte and had 15 assists at Golden State. He broke the franchise record with 128 steals.

While many of the league's rookies struggled late in the season, Hardaway played through the weariness and actually grew stronger, averaging 19.3 points, 8.2 assists, 6.6 rebounds and 2.1 steals in April. He was strong in the playoffs, too, even though the Magic were swept by Indiana in the first round. In those three playoff games, he averaged 44.3 minutes, 18.7 points, seven assists and 6.7 rebounds.

Penny often showed his frustration when things didn't go right, learning a hard lesson about the NBA. Playoff basketball was different than anything he had faced before. It was something that would prepare him for the following season. Because he despises losing, the sweep was especially painful. But it sent him home that summer with a new determination.

"I think we all saw the potential he has," said John Gabriel, Magic director of player personnel. "It won't be long before he becomes one of the most exciting players in the game."

G	FG-FGA	PCT	FT-FTA	PCT	REB-AVG	AST	PTS-AVG
82	509-1,092	.466	245-330	.742	439-5.4	544	1,313-16.0

1994-95

If Penny Hardaway's first season was a learning experience, his second season became his emergence as a true NBA star.

Hardaway began to blossom, taking the lessons he gained in his rookie season and converting them into confidence.

He improved his field-goal percentage (.512), his free-throw percentage (.769), his three-point shooting (.349), his assists average (7.2) and his scoring average (20.9). For his efforts, he was rewarded with his first All-Star appearance and a spot on the post-season All-NBA first team.

Prior to the season, the Magic traded point guard Scott Skiles, knowing Hardaway was ready to assume the role of playmaker for a budding team. He responded well, helping the Magic reach the NBA Finals in just their sixth season. But being swept by the Houston Rockets in the Finals soured Hardaway's great playoff performance. In 21 playoff games, he averaged 40.4 minutes, 19.6 points, 7.7 assists and 3.8 rebounds.

Hardaway kicked off his spectacular season by winning NBA Player of the Week honors late in November. Penny averaged 32.3 points, 6.5 rebounds, 6.5 assists, 2.5 steals and shot 56 percent from the field.

One of his brightest moments came against the Chicago Bulls when he scored a career-high 39 points, hitting the winning basket with 0.7 seconds remaining. In that game, he nailed 17 of 25 shots. Later in Boston, he dished out a career-high 19 assists.

He missed four games in April because of dehydration and inflammation of the esophagus, a condition which made it almost impossible for him to eat or drink. Without him, the Magic won only one of the four games, showing how important he was to the team and its championship hopes.

Hardaway earned his second career triple double when he recorded 35 points, 12 assists and 10 rebounds in 42 minutes at Milwaukee. Against Houston, the team that later would embarrass the Magic in the Finals, he

G	FG-FGA	PCT	FT-FTA	PCT	REB-AVG	AST	PTS-AVG
77	585-1,142	.512	356-463	.769	336-4.4	551	1,613-20.9

came away with a career-high seven steals.

Talk of whether the Magic made a smart draft-day trade in 1993 by getting Hardaway in exchange for Chris Webber, died quickly. Hardaway had become the real deal and the Orlando fans were happy.

1995-96

When Shaquille O'Neal fractured his thumb in the preseason, the prospects looked grim for the Orlando Magic — that is until Hardaway put the team on his back and carried the Magic early. He won the league's first Player of the Week and its first Player of the Month awards. He led the Magic to a 13-4 record in November, the best start in the NBA. They had forged a 17-5 record by the time O'Neal returned to the lineup. It was obvious that Hardaway had become their best player and arguably the best in the league.

sons, he played in all 82 games, priding himself on his durability. Despite a badly sprained ankle, he started one late-season game against Milwaukee and left after just three minutes. He insisted on starting to keep his streak alive.

He scored 30 points or more 14 times and distributed 10 or more assists 22 times. He joined Jordan on the All-NBA first team. While they started together in the backcourt for the Eastern Conference All-Star team, they also provided some memorable battles during the season.

G	FG-FGA	PCT	FT-FTA	PCT	REB-AVG	AST	PTS-AVG
82	623-1,215	.513	445-580	.767	354-4.3	582	1,780-21.7

He averaged 27 points, 6.5 assists and 5.8 rebounds in November. He also was learning how to score in the clutch. He hit three game-winning baskets in the closing seconds in the first seven weeks of the season.

He scored 42 points against New Jersey, including a bucket with 1.2 seconds remaining to win a triple-overtime war. Two weeks later, he hit a running, six-foot bank shot at the buzzer to beat Vancouver. And on Christmas Day, he beat Houston with an 11-foot jumper in traffic with 3.1 seconds left on the clock.

His scoring average climbed for his third consecutive season, rising to 21.7 points per game. He also averaged a team-best 7.1 assists per game. Penny's popularity continued to rise proportionately to the improvement of his game. He finished second only to Michael Jordan among guards in the Eastern Conference All-Star balloting.

For the second time in three sea-

Hardaway was crushed when the Magic were swept by the Bulls in the playoffs, vowing to become more of a leader in his fourth season. But that was before O'Neal left the team as a free agent.

Even so, Hardaway anxiously awaits his opportunity to assume full leadership of the Orlando Magic.

"He's the leader of this team, no question," Magic head coach Brian Hill says. "It's been that way for some time now. So much of the burden falls on his shoulders, and he handles it. There just isn't any phase of this game that he doesn't do well." •

Tim Povtak covers the Magic for The Orlando Sentinel.

PENNY by the numbers

Career Countdown

1   Hardaway's jersey number with the Orlando Magic

2   Triple doubles Hardaway's had in his pro career

3   Metatarsal bones fractured when Penny was shot in the foot while he was robbed during his freshman year at University of Memphis

4   Blocks Hardaway had against Portland (March 10, 1995), Detroit (Nov. 27, 1995) and Phoenix (Jan. 17, 1996) — his career best

5   Regular season games Penny has missed in his pro career

6   Votes separating Hardaway from '93-94 Rookie of the Year Chris Webber

7   Assists per game Hardaway has averaged in his pro career

8   Victories over nationally ranked teams for Memphis with Hardaway on the court

9   All-America selections Hardaway received at Memphis (Associated Press (2), *The Sporting News, Basketball Weekly*, U.S. Basketball Writers, John Wooden, Scripps-Howard, *Playboy, Basketball Times*)

10   NCAA postseason games Hardaway played in during two seasons at Memphis

11   Inches shorter Hardaway is than 7-6 Shawn Bradley, who was drafted one spot ahead of him at No. 2 in 1993

12   Points Hardaway scored in an 88-57 loss to Nick Van Exel's Cincinnati squad in the Midwest Region Finals of the NCAA Tournament on March 29, 1992 in Kansas City

13   Rebounds Hardaway had against Atlanta (Jan. 13, 1995) and Milwaukee (Feb. 4, 1994) — his career best

14   Games in which Hardaway scored 30 points or more in the 1995-96 season

BARRY GOSSAGE / NBA PHOTOS

15   Points per game Hardaway has scored as an All-Star*

16   Points per game Hardaway scored during his rookie season (1993-94)

17   Points Hardaway scored in his final college game, a 55-52 loss to Western Kentucky in the first round of the NCAA Tournament on March 8, 1993 in Orlando

18   Assists Hardaway has had as an All-Star*

19   Assists Hardaway had vs. Boston on April 13, 1995 — his career best

20   Points per game Hardaway scored in his two years at Memphis

21   Double doubles Hardaway had in the 1995-96 season

22   Points Hardaway scored in the 1994 Rookie All-Star Game, earning MVP honors

23   Games out of 32 that a Hardaway-led Orlando team has won without Shaquille

O'Neal in the lineup

24   Points Hardaway scored in a 83-79 overtime victory over Georgia Tech in the regional semifinals of the NCAA Tournament on March 27, 1992 in Kansas City

25   Hardaway's college jersey number (now retired) at Memphis

45   Three-point plays Penny completed in the 1995-96 season

107   Times Hardaway dunked in the 1995-96 season

210   Regular season games in which Hardaway has scored in double figures

3,039   Points Hardaway scored during his high school career at Memphis (Tenn.) Treadwell

4,706   Points Hardaway has scored in his 241 regular season games with the Magic

8,931   Minutes Hardaway has played in regular season games

* excludes 1994 Rookie All-Star Game

Career Stats

College (Memphis)

Year	G	FGM	FGA	PCT	FTM	FTA	PCT	REB	AVG	AST	AVG	PTS	AVG
91-92	34	209	483	.433	103	158	.652	237	7.0	188	5.5	590	17.4
92-93	32	249	522	.477	158	206	.767	273	8.5	204	6.4	729	22.8
Totals	66	458	1,005	.456	261	364	.717	510	7.7	392	5.9	1,319	20.0

Regular Season (NBA, Orlando Magic)

Year	G	FGM	FGA	PCT	FTM	FTA	PCT	REB	AVG	AST	AVG	PTS	AVG
93-94	82	509	1,092	.466	245	330	.742	439	5.4	544	6.6	1,313	16.0
94-95	77	585	1,142	.512	356	463	.769	336	4.4	551	7.2	1,613	20.9
95-96	82	623	1,215	.513	445	580	.767	354	4.3	582	7.1	1,780	21.7
Totals	241	1,717	3,449	.498	1,046	1,373	.762	1,129	4.7	1,677	7.0	4,706	19.5

Playoffs (NBA, Orlando Magic)

Year	G	FGM	FGA	PCT	FTM	FTA	PCT	REB	AVG	AST	AVG	PTS	AVG
93-94	3	22	50	.440	7	10	.700	20	6.7	21	7.0	56	18.7
94-95	21	144	305	.472	84	111	.757	79	3.8	162	7.7	412	19.6
95-96	12	101	217	.465	58	78	.744	56	4.6	72	6.0	280	23.3
Totals	36	267	572	.467	149	199	.749	155	4.3	255	7.1	748	20.7

Career Highs

Regular Season

Category	Total	Opponent	Date	Score
Points	42	New Jersey	Nov. 8, 1995	Orlando, 130-122 (3OT)
Rebounds	13	at Atlanta	Jan. 13, 1995	Orlando, 101-96
	13	Milwaukee	Feb. 4, 1994	Milwaukee, 98-92
Assists	19	at Boston	April 13, 1995	Boston, 119-114
Blocks	4	at Phoenix	Jan. 17, 1996	Orlando, 113-95
	4	Portland	March 10, 1995	Orlando, 97-85
Steals	7	Houston	Nov. 23, 1994	Orlando, 117-94

Playoff

Category	Total	Opponent	Date	Score
Points	38	Chicago	May 19, 1996	Chicago, 121-83
Rebounds	11	Atlanta	May 15, 1996	Orlando, 96-88
Assists	15	Indiana	May 25, 1995	Orlando, 119-114
Blocks	3	Boston	May 3, 1995	Orlando, 82-77
Steals	5	Chicago	May 7, 1995	Orlando, 94-91

All-Star Stats

Rookie All-Star Game

Year	MIN	FGM	FGA	PCT	FTM	FTA	PCT	REB	AST	PTS
1994*	22	8	9	.889	4	6	.667	1	3	22

* — Most Valuable Player

All-Star Game

Year	MIN	FGM	FGA	PCT	FTM	FTA	PCT	REB	AST	PTS
1995	31	4	9	.444	4	6	.667	5	11	12
1996	31	6	8	.750	4	4	1.000	3	7	18
Totals	62	10	17	.588	8	10	.800	8	18	30

penny's wild ride

A fictional look back at Penny Hardaway's career may provide more amusement than an entire theme park

By Tom D'Angelo

*b*efore we tour Miami's newest theme park, PennyLand, first some background on how a one-time NBA superstar parlayed a billion-dollar contract into one of the nation's most successful tourist attractions.

PennyLand is the creation of Penny Hardaway, sports' first billion-dollar baby. Hardaway played the first eight years of his 15-year career with the Orlando Magic (now the Orlando Magic Kingdom) before the team known then as the Miami Heat (now the Miami Carnival Cruiseliners) and its new owner Pat Riley lured Penny south.

See, Riley figured any player who scored 50 percent of his team's points was worth $1 billion for seven seasons.

But before we get ahead of ourselves, let's step back 12 years to 1996, when Penny was starting the third year of a paltry seven-year, $70 million contract. Of course, $70 million used to be a lot of money, but that was before teams like the New York Paramount Pictures started charging $10 million a season for front-row seats.

That season, Penny's former teammate (and new RCA/MGM/TBS/HBO owner) Shaquille O'Neal left Orlando for a meager $120 million. The then-Magic were stunned, and left with one half of the duo that was expected to lead Orlando to championship after championship into the next century. The Magic turned the team over to Hardaway, who, as Orlando's only star, became truly a one-man team.

Penny had little help back then. Horace Grant signed a five-year, $50 million deal that season, but he proved ineffective as the team's lone inside threat. Dennis Scott, so traumatized by his best friend's defection, protested by locking himself in Shaq's mansion and vowing not to come out until O'Neal returned to Orlando or shot 60 percent from the line, whichever came first.

Twelve years later, Scott has yet to emerge.

And the Magic, with little money to spend on free agents, settled for a center rotation of Geert Hammink, Joe Wolf, Robert Parish and Tree Rollins. Together, they averaged 1.4 points and 1.1 rebounds.

So as the Magic's win total declined, Penny's value increased. He became a permanent member of the league's All-Pro team and Central Florida's most popular figure without huge round ears.

Even averaging a triple double (as he did in 2000-01 while leading the league in scoring, rebounding and assists) didn't satisfy Penny. That season, Hardaway became a free agent, hoping somebody could squeeze him in under the $250 million salary cap.

Despite Miami's payroll of $35 bil-

penny vs. the greatest

How Hardaway's statistics compare to the numbers compiled by other celebrated guards after three seasons in the NBA:

Player	Age	Games	Assists	Avg.	Points	Avg.
Michael Jordan	24	182	911	5.0	5,762	31.7
Oscar Robertson	24	230	2,347	10.2	6,861	29.8
Jerry West	25	209	1,042	5.0	5,188	24.8
Pete Maravich	25	226	1,294	5.7	5,218	23.1
Isiah Thomas	23	235	2,113	9.0	4,827	20.5
Penny Hardaway	**24**	**241**	**1,677**	**7.0**	**4,706**	**19.5**
Bob Cousy	24	206	1,329	6.5	3,918	19.0
Magic Johnson	22	192	1,623	8.5	3,632	18.9
John Havlicek	25	235	616	2.6	4,110	17.5
John Stockton	25	246	1,695	6.9	1,736	7.1

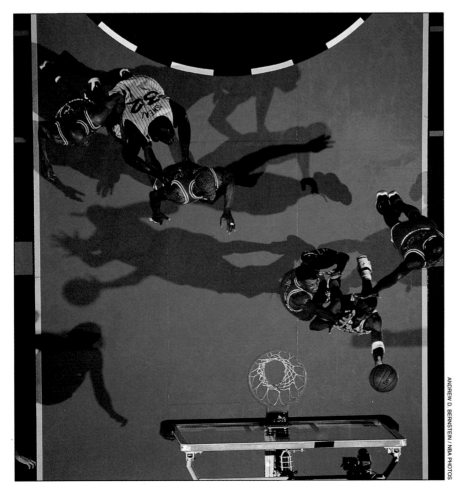

ANDREW D. BERNSTEIN / NBA PHOTOS

lion, Riley somehow was able to rescue Penny from Orlando. Penny was the final piece to Riley's plan to sign the rest of the league's All-Pro first team: Kobe Bryant, 5-year-old Kobe Bryant Jr., 42-year-old Magic Johnson and Lisa Leslie, the first woman to make the team. The deal was too good to be true: Penny's lone regret was never having the chance to play with Johnson, who retired for the 12th time following Penny's signing.

The only hitch in the negotiations was the signing of Orlando head coach Li'l Penny as a Miami assistant. Li'l Penny rose from being Penny's sidekick to Brian Hill's successor in Orlando.

Hill's departure was sealed when, in O'Neal's first game against his former team, the Magic head coach ordered his

In 1996, the Bulls knocked Penny's Magic out of the play-offs. But in 2006, Penny's Cruiseliners knocked the Bulls out of the record books.

team to foul Shaq on every play. The former Orlando center shot 70-for-350 from the line, and Orlando lost, 100-80.

That night, Hill began his postgame news conference by reiterating he and O'Neal never had a personality clash.

miami's big signings in 2001 started a string of seven consecutive championships for the Carnival Cruiseliners. Although he no longer was a one-man team, Hardaway's numbers continued to climb until he became the league's all-time scoring and assists leader.

The Cruiseliners averaged 75 victories during their championship run, and in 2005-06 won 80 games, obliterating the single-season record of 72 set by the team now known as the Chicago

Nikes, named after the company run by their new owner, Michael Jordan.

After seven consecutive titles and virtually every scoring and assist record, Penny decided to retire and open what would become one of the most popular vacation resorts.

The first attraction greeting the park's guests is a big ball called the Thriller Hill. Named after the man who coached Hardaway for the first four years of his career, the ride simulates an entire NBA season, going from city to city before an intense climb through the playoffs ends in a downhill series of sweeps.

The most popular novelty shop is Trader Shaq's, because of its low, low prices, which fluctuate with its namesake's free-throw shooting percentage. All items have been reduced to less than

wholesale rates.

Next to Trader Shaq's is the ride most enjoyed by hard-core capitalists: the Amway, a tribute to former Orlando Magic owner Rich DeVos. Distraught by O'Neal's decision to join the Lakers in 1996, DeVos later sold his two biggest companies, Amway Corporation and the Magic, to the Disney Corporation.

PennyLand's Amway is a wild ride that teaches customers how to make billions of dollars with one company and then lose their other company's biggest asset to a West Coast rival.

Penny had one wish before devoting his full attention to his flourishing theme park: to play one more game with the man to whom he was supposed to be linked for a generation.

Soon after he retired, Penny joined Shaq's World Tour for one game against Magic Johnson's 50-and-over team. Penny ended the game with 55 assists, each one going to Shaq, who called every play for himself and benched any player who dared shoot.

And the outcome wasn't much different from their final game together in Orlando. With his team trailing by only a point, Shaq insisted Penny not shoot an open layup so he could end the game with a dunk. Wilt Chamberlain, Johnson's 71-year-old center, fouled Shaq as the buzzer sounded. Shaq stepped to the line and both times . . . missed everything.

Hardaway smiled, remembering the good old days. •

Tom D'Angelo covers the Miami Heat for the Palm Beach *(Fla.)* Post.

penny's projections

Shaquille O'Neal's decision to join the Lakers could open new doors for Penny. Based on Penny's statistics in the 32 games he has played without Shaq in the lineup, Hardaway stands to put together an impressive Hall of Fame collection of stats as Orlando's only go-to guy.
Assuming Hardaway's career lasts 15 seasons, and based on his numbers with a Shaq-free lineup as well as his season averages for games played, Penny's projections place him in prestigious company:

Player (Seasons)	Games	Assists	Avg.	Rebs.	Avg.	Points	Avg.
Michael Jordan (13)*	928	5,300	5.7	5,900	6.3	29,673	32.0
Jerry West (14)	932	6,238	6.7	5,376	5.8	25,192	27.0
Penny Hardaway (15)*	**1,205**	**7,849**	**6.4**	**5,835**	**4.9**	**29,618**	**25.8**
Oscar Robertson (14)	1,040	9,887	9.5	7,804	7.5	26,710	25.7
Pete Maravich (10)	658	3,563	5.4	2,747	4.2	15,948	24.2
John Havlicek (16)	1,270	6,114	4.8	8,007	6.3	26,395	20.8
Magic Johnson (13)	906	10,141	11.2	6,559	7.2	17,707	19.5
Isiah Thomas (13)	979	9,061	9.3	3,478	3.6	18,822	19.2
Bob Cousy (14)	924	6,955	7.5	4,786	5.2	16,960	18.4
John Stockton (14)*	1,144	13,196	11.5	3,048	2.7	15,515	13.6

* projected

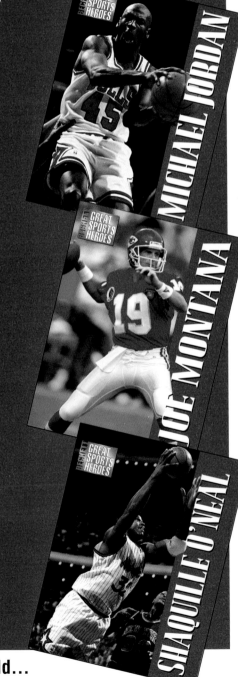